Essential Science Activities
for Key Stage 4

Examining GCSE Integrated Science
Barry Stone ● David Andrews ● Roy Williams

GCSE Physics for You
Keith Johnson

Examining GCSE Biology
Morton Jenkins ● Steven Bowden

Examining GCSE Chemistry
Bob McDuell

Problem-Solving in Science and Technology
David Rowlands

GCSE Biology Practical Assessment
David Newsham

GCSE Chemistry Practical Assessment
Brian Higginson

GCSE Physics Practical Assessment
Jim Breithaupt

Essential Science Activities
for Key Stage 4

Keith Bishop B.Sc. • **Bill Scott B.Sc., Ph.D.**
School of Education, University of Bath

David Maddocks B.Sc.
Information Technology Adviser for Durham
Education Authority

Stanley Thornes (Publishers) Ltd

First Published in 1990 by:
Stanley Thornes (Publishers) Ltd
Old Station Drive
Leckhampton
CHELTENHAM GL53 0DN
England

British Library Cataloguing in Publication Data
Bishop, Keith
    Essential science activities for key stage 4.
    1. Science
    I. Title II. Maddocks, David III. Scott, William
    500

    ISBN 0–7487–0429–9

Front cover illustrations

Spray of glass fibre optics consisting of 2000 individual strands each measuring 60 microns thick. This type of cable is used for decorative lighting.
Adam Hart-Davis/Science Photo Library

'Cold Fusion': French CEA experimental apparatus used to investigate the results of Fleischmann & Pons, who, in March 1989, claimed to have created sustained cold fusion energy production in a simple electrolytic cell.
Philippe Plailly/Science Photo Library

Slash and burn agriculture, Amazon Basin, Peru.
Paul Franklin/Oxford Scientific Films

Back cover illustration

False-colour scanning electron micrograph (SEM) of velcro. A common fastener, velcro is a nylon material manufactured in two separate pieces, one with a hooked surface (right) and the other with a smooth surface covered with loops (left).
Magnification: ×40.
Dr Jeremy Burgess/Science Photo Library

Line artwork by Nick Hawken

Typeset by Opus, Oxford

Printed and bound in Great Britain by Martin's of Berwick

Contents

Practicals

Attainment Target 11: Electricity and Magnetism

Attainment Target 13: Energy

Attainment Target 14: Sound and Music

Attainment Target 15: Using Light and Electromagnetic Radiation

Attainment Target 16: The Earth in Space

Attainment Target 17: The Nature of Science

Introduction

This Resource Pack comprises a set of **Exercises** and a set of **Practicals** linked closely to the **Attainment Levels** within **Attainment Targets 2–17** for **National Curriculum Science, Key Stage 4**.

Exercises

Sixty-one exercises have been designed to provide data and information on new developments in science and technology. The Exercises are tailored closely to the recommendations spelled out within the National Curriculum with the aim of widening the range of new situations in which students can practise applying their scientific knowledge. Most Exercises are within reach of the average student, and in addition there are many which will stretch the more able.

Practicals

Fifty-one Practicals provide new material and novel perspectives on familiar activities to meet the demands for the National Curriculum as directly as possible. It is important to note that some Attainment Targets lend themselves to practical work more readily than others.

K. Bishop, W. Scott, D. Maddocks

Essential Science Activities and the National Curriculum

Attainment Target	Exercise/Practical Number and Title		4	5	6	7	8	9	10
2: The Variety of Life	E1	The Nitrogen Cycle				●			
	E2	Food Webs		●	●	●			
	E3	Adapted to Cities			●				
	E4	Biological Control							●
	E5	Population Studies						●	
	E6	Food Chains		●					
	P1	Treating Used Water					●		
	P2	Effects of a Sewage Works					●		
	P3	Investigating Microbes in Water					●		
3: Processes of Life	E7	Organ Systems					●		
	E8	Diabetes and Blood Sugar						●	
	E9	Medical Technology					●		
	E10	Food and Diet			●				
	E11	Food Additives (1)				●			
	E12	Food Additives (2)				●			
	E13	Disability		●					
	E14	AIDS					●		
	E15	Heart Trouble					●		
	E16	Photosynthesis						●	
	P4	Digesting Food				●			
	P5	Photosynthesis						●	
	P6	Sensory Games (1) – Sight				●			
	P7	Sensory Games (2) – Hearing				●			
	P8	Sensory Games (3) – Touch				●			
	P9	Sensory Games (4) – Taste and Smell				●			
	P10	Growth of Plants				●			
	P11	Separating Colours in Plants						●	
	P12	Investigating Water in Food		●					
	P13	Investigating Vitamin C		●					
4: Genetics and Evolution	E17	Abortion					●		
	E18	Test-tube Babies					●	●	●
	E19	Colour Blind?					●	●	●
	E20	Blood Groups					●	●	●
5: Human Influences on the Earth	E21	Global Warming						●	
	E22	Pollution of the North Sea						●	
	E23	Stubble Burning							●
	E24	Maps of the World				●			
	E25	Going, Going ...					●		
	P14	Clean Air from Power Stations					●		
	P15	Treading on Grass				●			
6: Types and Uses of Materials	E26	Metal Resources							●
	E27	Discovering Resources				●			
	P16	Displacement Reactions			●				
	P17	Packets of Milk					●		
	P18	Investigating Tea-bags					●		
7: Making New Materials	E28	Polymers						●	
	E29	Rubber						●	
	E30	Bonding							●
	P19	Salt and the Enzyme in Saliva				●			
	P20	The Effect of Enzymes on Proteins				●			
	P21	Reaction and Concentration					●		
	P22	Indigestion				●			
	P23	Preserving Food (Part 1)				●			
	P24	Preserving Food (Part 2)				●			
	P25	Why do Apples go Brown when Cut?			●				
	P26	Investigating the Freshness of Milk				●			
	P27	Protecting Materials				●			

Attainment Target	Exercise/Practical Number and Title	4	5	6	7	8	9	10
8: Explaining How Materials Behave	E31 Half-life						•	
	E32 Isotopes					•		
	E33 Sweating				•	•	•	•
	E34 Food Irradiation						•	
	P28 Radioactivity and Living Things						•	
	P29 Getting into Hot Water			•				
9: Earth and Atmosphere	E35 Sunshine Recording			•				
	P30 Limestone			•				
	P31 Hard Rocks		•					
10: Forces	E36 Accident Recoil							•
	E37 Stopping				•			
	P32 Bones as Levers			•				
	P33 Modelling Paper Bones		•					
	P34 The Efficiency of Pulleys				•			
11: Electricity and Magnetism	E38 Power Generation					•	•	
	E39 The Right Fuse			•				
	E40 Electricity Bills			•				
	E41 Conductors					•		
	E42 Investigating a Circuit					•		
	P35 Investigating Batteries		•					
	P36 Fire Alarm Circuit		•					
	P37 Magnetic Effect of an Electric Current				•			
	P38 Eddy Currents				•			
12: Information Technology	E43 Codes			•				
	E44 Bar Codes			•				
	E45 Logic Gates (1)				•			
	E46 Logic Gates (2)				•			
13: Energy	E47 Energy Sources		•					
	E48 Storage Heaters				•			
	E49 New Wave Power					•		
	E50 Energy Conservation							•
	E51 Measuring Food Energy				•			
	E52 In the Gym						•	
	P39 Storing Heat				•			
	P40 Energy From Chemicals	•						
	P41 Releasing Heat Energy					•		
	P42 Measuring Energy in Food					•		
14: Sound and Music	E53 Comparing Sounds			•				
	E54 Samplers					•	•	
	P43 Investigating Stereo			•				
15: Using Light and Electro-magnetic Radiation	E55 Fibre Optics				•			
	E56 Colour TV				•			
	E57 Cat's-eyes			•				
	E58 Roasting in the Sun				•			
	P44 The Rainbow Effect			•				
	P45 Colour TV				•			
	P46 Sight Defects			•				
	P47 Investigating Sunglasses			•				
	P48 Investigating Polarised Light							•
16: The Earth in Space	E59 Speed of Light			•				
	E60 Other Planets			•				
	P49 Measuring the Moon			•				
17: The Nature of Science	E61 Cold Fusion					•		
	P50 Making Observations		•					
	P51 Gathering Evidence and Drawing Conclusions			•				

Acknowledgements

The authors and publisher are grateful to the following for permission to reproduce material:

Ardea, Exercise 19
Avon Gymnasium Manufacturing Co. Ltd, Exercise 52
Biophotos, Exercise 3
Environmental Picture Library, Exercise 29
Greenpeace, Practical 1 (right)
The Guardian, Exercises 15 and 23
Hydro-Electric, Exercise 49
The Observer, Exercise 49
Carmela Rodger, Exercise 13
Science Photo Library, Practical 62
Severn Trent Water, Practical 1 (left)
SWEB, Exercise 48

Every effort has been made to contact copyright holders and we apologise if any have been overlooked.

Attainment
Target 2
**THE VARIETY
OF LIFE**

Level 6

EXERCISE 1

The Nitrogen Cycle

The Agriculture and Food Research Council has said that the nitrate levels in the water supply have been allowed to build up since the Second World War. Nitrate levels are so high in some parts of Britain that underground aquifers have been sealed off to prevent the contamination of tap water supplies. Somewhere between ten and thirty per cent of the 1.6 million tonnes of nitrogen fertiliser that British farmers spread in 1987 was lost either into the atmosphere or by leaching into the water supply.

Why should nitrate levels be cause for concern? Nitrate pollution is suspected of being connected with the incidence of stomach cancer and with 'blue baby' births.

The World Health Organisation (WHO) recommendations set a limit of 100 mg of nitrates per litre of water from agricultural run-off, whereas the European Community (EC) has set a much lower limit of 50 mg per litre.

⇨ **1** The diagram on this page shows a way of illustrating the nitrogen cycle. Look at it carefully and draw arrows 1, 2, 8, 10, 12 and 13 in their correct places.

2 Write a short explanation of what is happening for arrows 4, 6, 7 and 11.

3 On the diagram mark the pathways showing where nitrates come from and how they reach us.

4 It is suggested that even if farmers stop spreading nitrogen-containing fertiliser tomorrow the nitrate problem will not go away for years. Why is this?

5 The WHO and the EC have recommended quite different limits for the amount of nitrate that should be allowed into public water supplies. What reasons can you suggest for this difference?

6 Organic fertiliser spread in the form of manure or compost does not release nitrates into the soil water as quickly as inorganic fertiliser such as ammonium nitrate. Explain this and write an argument for organic farming. Are there any drawbacks?

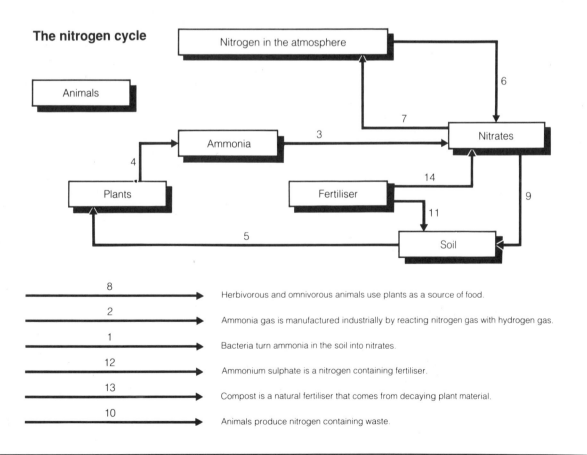

The nitrogen cycle

8 — Herbivorous and omnivorous animals use plants as a source of food.

2 — Ammonia gas is manufactured industrially by reacting nitrogen gas with hydrogen gas.

1 — Bacteria turn ammonia in the soil into nitrates.

12 — Ammonium sulphate is a nitrogen containing fertiliser.

13 — Compost is a natural fertiliser that comes from decaying plant material.

10 — Animals produce nitrogen containing waste.

EXERCISE 2

Food Webs

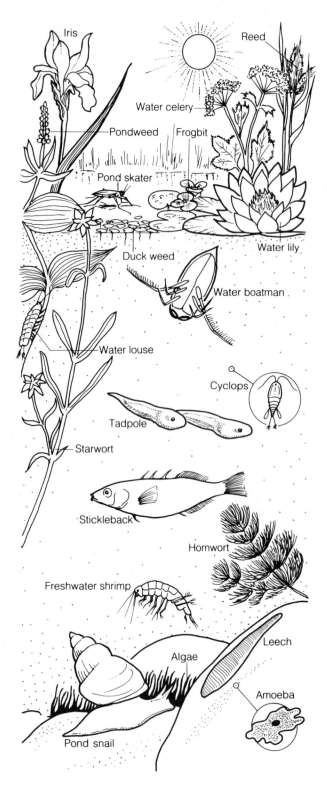

The pupils at Rowchester Comprehensive School had been told they could go ahead and build their pond on a piece of unused land on the edge of the school grounds. It was part of a GCSE ecology project designed to get them to use ecological principles and terms. They designed the pond on paper and decided what plants and animals to introduce to the pond. This sketch gives some idea of how the environment looked after a couple of years.

▷ **1** What kind of ecosystem have the pupils created?

2 The ecosystem is made up of two communities; the plant community and the animal community. Look at the picture and separate the organisms into plants and animals.

3 From the picture decide which plants are:
a) floating, b) submerged, c) semi-submerged.

4 Identify the carnivores and herbivores amongst the animals.

5 From the plants and animals in the picture write out as many food chains as you can. Then use those food chains to make a food web for the pond. A food web shows the feeding relationships between the organisms. You will have to use reference books to find out what the different organisms feed on.

6 Choose one of the organisms, plant or animal, and with the help of reference books describe its ecological niche.

7 An ecosystem is determined by the combination of living (biotic) and non-living (abiotic) factors. A table of of these two groups of factors has been started below. Using the information in the picture, complete a table of your own.

	biotic	*abiotic*
1	floating plants	water temperature

Attainment
Target 2
**THE VARIETY
OF LIFE**

Level 6

EXERCISE 3

Adapted to Cities

The ways in which organisms are adapted to particular habitats can sometimes be of use to us. Lichens are very sensitive to changes in environmental conditions. They are unusual because they are biological marriages between two plants, an alga and a fungus.

Lichens are quick to absorb pollutants in the atmosphere and are particularly sensitive to sulphur dioxide. They follow this pattern:

sensitivity to SO_2 ↑   stringy lichens

            leafy lichens

            powdery lichens

Xanthoria parietina

Parmelia saxatilis

Cladonia arbuscula

▷ **1** The sensitivity of lichens is thought to be related to their form or shape. Look at the photos of the three different types and suggest what the link might be.

2 *Lecanora muralis* is a powdery lichen which is quite damaging to buildings. Gradually, as other lichens disappear, it is taking a grip on many buildings in cities with large numbers of cars. Explain what is going on and what needs to be done to reverse the trend.

3 Lichens can be used as a means of monitoring pollution control by transplanting them from other areas. Which kinds of lichens would be used and what is the theory behind this idea? Explain why lichens are now being called biomonitors.

4 *Parmelia saxatalis* is now thriving in some city centres where pedestrianisation has taken place. Explain what has been happening.

5 After the atomic bomb tests in the 1950s, which sent all kinds of radioactive materials into the upper atmosphere, reindeer bones were found to contain high concentrations of the radioisotopes Caesium-137 and Strontium-90. Reindeer have a mixed vegetarian diet and live in fairly unpolluted areas of the world. Explain what has been happening.

6 Lichens are good examples of organisms showing symbiotic relationships. What is symbiosis and how might the relationship between the alga and the fungus be working?

Attainment
Target 2
**THE VARIETY
OF LIFE**

Level 10

EXERCISE 4

Biological Control

Organic farming does not allow the use of pesticides to protect crops from damage. In 1989 there was another massive explosion in the population of aphids (blackfly and greenfly), the highest for 15 years.

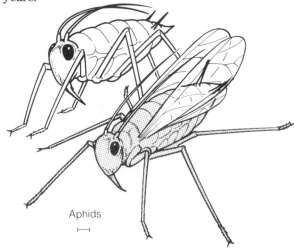

Aphids

While other farmers can use chemical pesticides, organic farmers have a problem. The organic farmer, therefore, must rely on biological control.

These animals are all predators of aphids. The relationship between these organisms and the aphid is known as a predator–prey relationship.

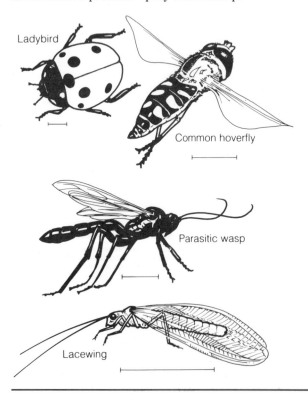

Ladybird

Common hoverfly

Parasitic wasp

Lacewing

In other managed environments there may not be a natural predator present in great enough numbers, in which case a predator may have to be introduced. Sometimes the consequences of the introduction of a foreign species can be quite disastrous.

1 Using reference books, find out the life cycle of the aphid and draw a diagram to represent it.

2 What is the feeding method of aphids? Draw a diagram of the mouthparts to show what it does.

3 The graph below shows the predator–prey relationship between aphids and ladybirds. Explain why the peaks occur at different times and why both populations eventually decline.

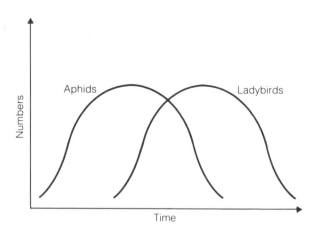

4 Aphids can reproduce by a process of asexual reproduction called parthenogenesis. Find out what asexual and parthenogenesis mean and explain what the advantages are for the aphid in being able to do this.

5 The coypu has just been eradicated from the Norfolk Broads after many years. What is a coypu, why was it introduced in the first place and why did it become a pest?

6 Use a reference library to find other examples of biological control where the predator is a foreign species which has been specially introduced. Say whether the introduction has been successful or not. If not, what were the consequences?

7 Try to find out how genetic engineering is being used to create micro-organisms which can be used in the biological control of fungi.

EXERCISE 5

Population Studies

The two graphs show the ages of the people living in two countries. The vertical axis of each graph shows different age groups. The horizontal axis shows the percentage of the population in each age group in each country.

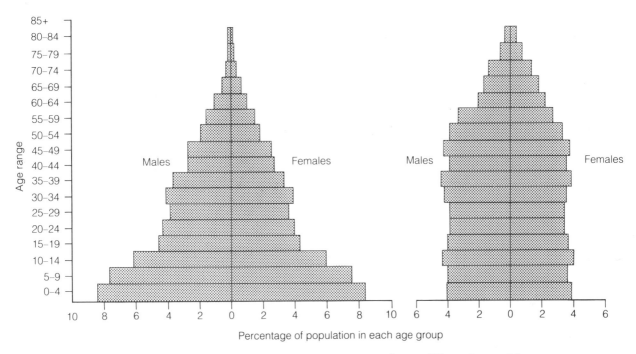

Population graphs showing the age structure of two different countries

1 Imagine that you are describing these two graphs in a telephone conversation. Write down what you would say. You should mention anything that you think is important but you must say something about the birth rate, the female : male ratio and the number of people over 64 in each population.

2 One of the graphs is of a developed country and one is of a less developed country. Decide which is which and give your reasons for making the choice.

3 Draw a histogram showing the ratio of people: under 16, between 16 and 64 and over 64 for each population. Why do you think these three age groups were chosen?

4 Sketch the shape that the two population graphs might have in 40 years time. Make the following assumptions:

for the less developed country
(a) the birth rate goes on increasing at the same rate for 20 years and then stays steady
(b) the death rate amongst young children falls by 10% a year.

for the developed country
(a) the birth rate stays the same for 20 years and then increases steadily
(b) medical advances mean that more people live longer.

5 For each of the populations in 40 years time, say how the number of live births is likely to differ from the number of children who live to the age of five. Explain your answer.

EXERCISE 6

Food Chains

Vegetarians would argue that it is wasteful to grow crops in order to feed them to animals which in turn are slaughtered for us to eat. They say that each link in the food chain decreases the efficiency of the process.

The eagle eats the rabbit but only 10% of the energy absorbed by the eagle turns into eagle flesh.

2% of sunlight produces new grass.

Only 30% of the new grass is eaten by the herbivores.

The energy that is used to grow food comes from the sun. However not all the sun's energy falling onto the earth is used. Think of a meadow where the grass is being grazed by rabbits, which are then preyed upon by eagles.

⇨ **1** Write down three food chains showing examples of what vegetarians mean by a decrease in efficiency.

2 Write a food chain to represent the relationships between the plant and animal organisms shown in the drawing.

3 Identify the herbivore and carnivore shown in the drawing.

Imagine that 5000 million joules (5 gigajoules) of energy fall on to a half hectare pasture in a year.

4 How many joules' worth of grass does this produce?

5 How many joules' worth of rabbit does this produce?

6 If 1% of the rabbits are taken by eagles, how many joules of flesh will the eagles eat?

7 How many joules do you think will find their way into the eagles' flesh?

8 What happens to the rest of the energy (90%) absorbed by the rabbit? (There are two major uses.)

9 What do you think happens to the rest of the grass?

10 Some of the light energy falling on the grass is reflected, some is absorbed by the soil, some is used to evaporate moisture from the grass. Estimate the percentage of energy used for each of these three activities. (Remember the total = 98%)

EXERCISE 7

Organ Systems

The human body is a living machine made up of organ systems which work together. They communicate with one another through the nervous and endocrine systems.

This flow diagram shows how the different systems work together to make saliva.

⇨ Draw similar flow diagrams to show how organ systems can work together when you:
   (a) sweat
   (b) jump with fright
   (c) blink
   (d) put on warmer clothes because you feel cold
   (e) do an emergency stop in a car.

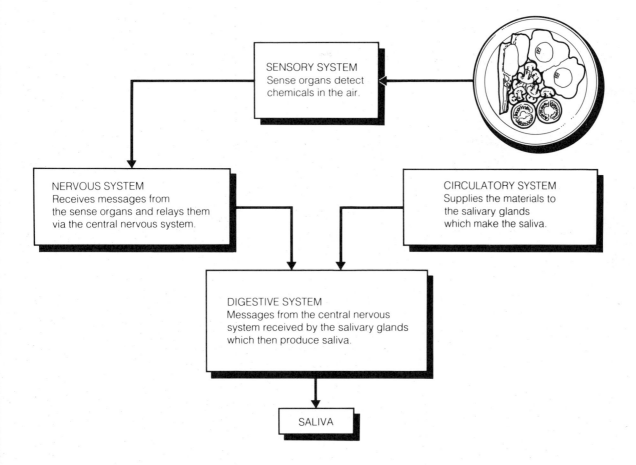

SENSORY SYSTEM
Sense organs detect chemicals in the air.

NERVOUS SYSTEM
Receives messages from the sense organs and relays them via the central nervous system.

CIRCULATORY SYSTEM
Supplies the materials to the salivary glands which make the saliva.

DIGESTIVE SYSTEM
Messages from the central nervous system received by the salivary glands which then produce saliva.

SALIVA

EXERCISE 8

Diabetes and Blood Sugar

There are about a million people in the UK with diabetes. Diabetics are people who have insufficient, ineffective or a total lack of a hormone called insulin. The importance of insulin is that it controls the level of glucose in the blood.

As food is digested glucose is released into the bloodstream. If the glucose level is too high it can lead to damage to the eyes and kidneys and increases the risk of heart disease. If the level is too low it can result in dizziness and eventually loss of consciousness.

In people who produce insulin normally the changes in glucose levels are minimised. This process where the human body tries to maintain steady conditions is called homeostasis.

The table below gives gives the figures obtained when blood glucose level was monitored over a 12-hour period. Normal blood glucose level is about 100 mg per 100 cm^3.

Time (hr)	0600	0700	0800	0845	0900	1000	1100	1130
Blood sugar (mg/100 cm^3)	100	100	130	145	138	106	85	74

Time (hr)	1200	1300	1330	1400	1500	1600	1700	1800
Blood sugar (mg/100 cm^3)	70	86	100	111	111	102	97	101

⇨ **1** Draw a graph of blood sugar (mg per 100 cm^3) against time (h).

2 On your graph mark when you think the following events took place:
   (a) a carbohydrate rich meal was eaten in the morning
   (b) insulin was released into the blood after this meal
   (c) exercise was started and finished in the morning
   (d) a snack was eaten at lunchtime.

3 Explain why the glucose level dropped for a while after exercise.

4 No food was eaten between breakfast and lunch yet the blood glucose level still rose to return to normal. Where did this glucose come from?

5 Use the set of figures to explain the meaning of the term homeostasis.

There are two types of diabetes.

Insulin dependent diabetes (IDD). These diabetics have lost the ability to produce insulin and are usually diagnosed at a young age. They need insulin injections to control the blood glucose level.

Non-insulin dependent diabetes (NIDD). This condition usually affects older people. They can control their diabetes through diet or with the help of tablets. They do not need insulin injections.

6 Explain why the following points are important for any diabetic person to consider:
   (a) the timing of meals
   (b) the size of meals
   (c) the types of foods to eat
   (d) the taking of exercise.

7 A 'hypo', (hypoglycaemic reaction), can occur if injected insulin has no glucose to act on. The symptoms are dizziness and loss of consciousness in extreme cases. Find out the circumstances in which this could occur, how it can be avoided and what to do if it does happen.

Attainment
Target 3
**PROCESSES
OF LIFE**

Level 8

EXERCISE 9

Medical Technology

Thirty years ago everyone with permanent kidney failure died, but now medical technology has developed to a point where difficult choices have to be made. The two commonest forms of treatment are regular dialysis or transplant surgery, both of which are expensive and limited. Doctors therefore have to make life and death decisions about who should be treated; but on what basis?

In 1985 the British Medical Journal published results of a survey of doctors which asked about the criteria used for deciding who should be recommended for dialysis treatment. The questionnaire outlined the medical and social backgrounds of 16 fictitious patients and asked more than 700 doctors to rank them in order of priority for treatment. These were the results:

Rank	Type of person
1	55-year-old woman with asthma
2	72-year-old male vet
3	36-year-old man with paraplegia
4	53-year-old male diabetic
5	59-year-old female diabetic
6	25-year-old blind male diabetic
7	62-year-old man with stroke
8	49-year-old woman with rheumatoid arthritis
9	50-year-old educationally sub-normal woman
10	45-year-old female analgesic abuser
11	67-year-old Asian with no English
12	51-year-old woman with breast cancer
13	50-year-old man with Ischaemic heart disease
14	30-year-old man with schizophrenia
15	52-year-old male alcoholic
16	29-year-old hepatitis B positive man

⇨ **1** What criteria do you think the doctors used to make their choices?

2 From the list does it seem that medical or social reasons were the basis of the doctors' choices?

3 Do you agree with this rank order?
Discuss these ideas and agree on an order. Write down your reasons.

4 Find out what dialysis is and how peritoneal dialysis differs from the use of a kidney machine.

Transplant surgery

Read the following extract carefully and answer the questions that follow. You will have to do some personal research to answer them all.

Unless individuals are genetically identical the body's immune system rejects tissue from other people as 'foreign'. But this has been largely overcome by powerful anti-rejection drugs. Particularly successful is cyclosporin A of which only low doses are needed leading to success rates of 85 per cent or more.

In the UK in 1987 over 1600 kidneys were transplanted, but this success is now causing another problem; that of supply. For transplants to take place donor organs are needed, and this has led to a new and rather unfortunate trade in human kidneys. There have been cases recently where poor but healthy people have sold one of their kidneys for transplantation into wealthy but ailing recipients. Up until now organ donation has always been accepted amongst close relatives but this development raises many new moral and ethical issues. Establishing that there is a family relationship between donor and recipient can be done by genetic fingerprinting but this may not necessarily prevent exploitation.

5 Explain why successful transplant surgery between unrelated people requires the use of anti-rejection drugs, whereas they may not be needed for transplants between genetic relatives.

6 Do you think there should be a legal restriction requiring a donor to be a genetic relative of the recipient, bearing in mind that this will probably restrict the supply of kidneys for transplants?

7 Would your answer to Q6 prevent husbands, wives or close friends offering to be donors?

8 Find out how genetic fingerprinting could prevent a commercial trade in organs such as kidneys.

Attainment
Target 3
**PROCESSES
OF LIFE**

Level 6

EXERCISE 10

Food and Diet

Even today you still hear the phrase, 'a calorie controlled diet' and you will often find the energy values of foods still given in calories. The term calorie is actually shorthand for kilocalorie (kcal) but it is now being replaced by kilojoule (kJ). Look on the label of any packeted food and you will find both kcal and kJ. Eventually kcal will be phased out so you need to get used to using kJ.

Look at the table of figures and convert the kcal energy value into kJ by multiplying by 4.2. The first one has been done already.

Food (100 g)	Energy value (kcal)	Energy value (kJ)
cheddar cheese	410	1722
fish fingers	190	
butter	750	
green pepper	20	
boiled potatoes	80	
chips	230	
apple	50	
wholemeal bread	240	

To calculate the energy value of a food you need to know the following information:

• mass of the food (g),
• mass of surrounding water (kg),
• specific heat capacity of water,
• rise in temperature of the water (°C).

The specific heat capacity of water is approximately

$$4.2 \text{ kJ/kg/}^\circ\text{C}$$

This table shows some of the results of bomb calorimeter experiments.

Food	Mass burnt (g)	Mass of water (kg)	Rise in water temperature (°C)
carrot	10	0.5	4
banana	20	1.0	16
lentils	5	0.5	30
margarine	1	1.0	8

Use this pattern to do the following calculations.

Energy value of food = (kJ)

$$\frac{\text{mass of water} \times 4.2 \times \text{temperature rise in water}}{\text{(kg)} \qquad \qquad (^\circ\text{C})}$$

1 Work out the energy value of each food.

2 You will have noticed that the foods do not have the same mass. Carry out further calculations to find out the energy value of:
(a) 10 g of each food
(b) 100 g of each food.

3 Now present the figures in the form of a table:

Food	Mass (g)	Energy value (kJ)	Energy value (kJ per 10 g)	Energy value (kJ per 100 g)

4 Find out what mass of these foods you might eat in one go. In other words calculate the energy value of a banana or a carrot or the amount of margarine you might spread on a slice of bread.

5 Find a nutritional chart from a magazine or a text book and calculate the energy value in kJ of a typical main meal. You will have to estimate, or better still, measure the mass of the food before you eat it!

Attainment
Target 3
**PROCESSES
OF LIFE**

Level 7

EXERCISE 11

Food Additives (1)

Many processed foods contain additives. By law these have to be listed on the packet, and many have E-numbers so that people know what they are buying. Some of the main additives are shown on this sheet.

E 100–180 Food colours

Colours are used to brighten up processed foods. The addition of colour ensures a standard appearance which many consumers now expect. Bright colours also make confectionery attractive to children.

The colours marked* are synthetic (do not occur naturally).

E 101	riboflavin (vitamin B2)	yellow
E 102*	tartrazine	yellow
E 110*	sunset yellow	orange
E 123*	amaranth	red
E 131*	patent blue	blue
E 132*	indigo	blue
E 141	chlorophyll	green
E 150	caramel	brown
E 162	beetroot extract	red
E 163	anthocyanins	purple

E 102 (tartrazine) can be found in all kinds of packet and convenience foods. It can cause allergic reactions in some hypersensitive people, particularly those with a history of asthma or eczema.

E 200–297 Preservatives

Preservatives are used to inhibit the growth of fungi and bacteria which would spoil the food. Eating food in which these micro-organisms have multiplied can cause anything from a slight stomach upset to death.

There are a number of traditional ways of preserving food, like bottling, pickling, salting, smoking and drying. Chemical preservatives are used as a cheap way of keeping food fresh longer.

A lot of preservatives occur naturally, but generally they are produced synthetically.

E200	sorbic acid
E210	benzoic acid and benzoates
E220–227	sulphur dioxide
E249–252	nitrites and nitrates
E260	acetic acid
E296	malic acid

E 249–252 (nitrates and nitrites) are used to preserve meat products. The nitrite is responsible for inhibiting the growth of the bacterium that causes botulism. The amount of nitrite in food is carefully controlled because there is a possibility that it will combine with certain compounds in the body to form cancer producing agents called nitrosamines.

E 300–321 Anti-oxidants

The use of anti-oxidants is a cheap way to prevent the break down of food fats which occurs when food is exposed to heat, light, water or contact with metals. Oxygen in the atmosphere combines with the fats, makes the food smell and taste rancid and forms compounds which may be harmful.

E 300	ascorbic acid (vitamin C)
E 306–308	tocopherols (vitamin E)
E 320–321	BHA and BHT

E 321 (butylated hydroxy toluene) is a common additive in margarines. Some people are sensitive to BHT and may develop skin rashes.

E 322–500 Emulsifiers and Stabilisers

This is a broad group of additives which are used to alter or maintain the texture of certain manufactured foods. Many of these are in fact natural plant or animal products.

Emulsifiers are used to create a uniform texture in the product where fats and water are present together.

Stabilisers work with emulsifiers to improve the texture of the product.

E 322	lecithin; emulsifier (natural substance)
E 330	citric acid; stabiliser (natural substance)
E 420	sorbitol; sweetener (natural substance)
E 440	pectin; gelling agent (natural substance)
E 450	phosphate; many uses

E 450 (phosphates and polyphosphates) are used mainly in cooked meat and chicken products where they help to retain water. Regulations control the amount of this very expensive water which manufacturers can sell to the consumer.

▷ **1** What goes into your food?
In the next week collect labels and packets from food used at home and bring them into school.
2 Design a table which classifies the foods and the additives they contain.
3 In your groups make a display of these to show which additives are used and why?
4 Compare your displays and decide whose display is the clearest.
5 Find out which foods still contain E 102. Then look for similar foods from other manufacturers to see if it has been replaced by 'natural colours' such as carotene.

Attainment
Target 3
**PROCESSES
OF LIFE**

Level 7

EXERCISE 12

Food Additives (2)

Do additives in food arouse strong feelings in you? Do we need additives in our food? What are additives? Who do you believe when different groups of people with different interests tell you different things?

Here are five statements from various people putting forward their opinions about additives in food. They have been brought together to discuss the statement that, 'additive concoctions should be banned from sale'.

The Nutritionist
Food itself is only a concoction of chemicals. Additives are also chemicals so why shouldn't we use them? There are cases where the balance of the risk of eating additives as opposed to the risk of getting food poisoning lies in favour of the additives. The rule surely is don't use additives where they cannot be justified on grounds of health and safety. Adding colours, for instance, is only a matter of fashion. As long as the consumer has been educated about the possible risks of some of the synthetic colours, and the products are clearly labelled, the choice should lie with the consumer. The danger is that the public will continue to be influenced by the attractiveness of the product and not by its nutritional value.

The Superstore Manager
Well packaged foods of consistent quality have a long shelf life and are easy to handle. Additives reduce the risk of food poisoning and make the product attractive to the consumer. We feel we should be supplying what the consumer demands. If tastes change and additive-free foods are demanded then we will stock additive-free foods. The danger we see lies in unscrupulous manufacturers who use additives to compensate for low quality raw materials.

The Food Manufacturer
The use of additives helps to keep prices down. Products have a longer shelf life and are of consistent quality. Additives make food safer. The public is still largely unaware of the rules of food hygiene. The risks from additives are smaller than the risks from food poisoning.

The Consumer
The sort of thing I want to know is, will eating a certain additive-containing food so many times a week for so many years eventually give me cancer?
Which additives are safe and which aren't? Who do I believe?
I think the government, schools and consumer organisations should be responsible for educating the public so that we can make informed choices.

The Green Consumer
Colour additives are pointless. Natural colours are equally good, if you accept that they are not so bright and garish.
Preservatives such as sulphur dioxide, nitrates and nitrites should be banned. I believe the health risk from these additives is greater than the risk of getting food poisoning.
Anti-oxidants such as the benzoates are derived from known carcinogens and should be banned. I avoid all additive concoctions such as pot soups and synthetic creams. They are nutritionally valueless.

▷ *Use their statements to help you form a discussion group.* The nutritionist has been asked to chair the meeting. It needs a secretary to take the minutes of the meeting. The agenda for the meeting is as follows.

1 Bacon and pot soups are examples of products which should be banned from sale.

2 E numbers are a useful means of controlling the use of additives in food.

3 Education is the best way of enabling the public to make informed choices about the food they buy.

4 Manufacturers say that food will become more expensive if additives are banned.

EXERCISE 13

Disability

In September 1988 the Office of Population Censuses and Surveys (OPCS) published a report designed to present a complete picture of disablement amongst adults in Great Britain. The last national survey was carried out in 1969 when it was estimated that there were about 3 million disabled adults. The present survey includes almost 4.3 million people aged over 60.

It is a matter of controversy whether elderly people should be automatically included in the survey. One side of the argument says that many elderly people would not class themselves as disabled as they would expect relatively minor limitations of movement, hearing or vision to be normal for their age. The Disability Alliance representing more than 100 groups disagrees, saying that pensioners with disabilities should be included.

(The Prevalence of Disability Among Adults: OPCS Surveys of Disability in Great Britain Report 1. HMSO 1988)*

Wheelchair athlete

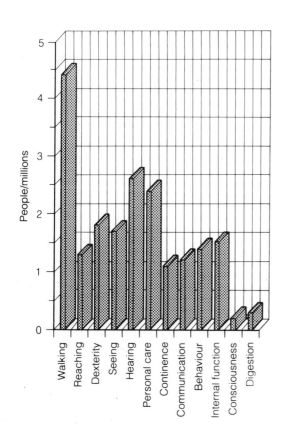

Disability among adults in the UK

▷ **1** Make a list of the different classes of disability by putting them into rank order according to their numbers.

2 From the graph work out the total number of disabilities.

3 It is unlikely that this number is the same as the number of disabled people in Great Britain. Give at least two reasons to explain why this is so.

4 Find out from a reference book what is meant by the terms:

● dexterity
● continence
● internal function
● personal care
● communication.

5 Ageing is a process which, by its very nature, is likely to lead to some physical or mental limitations in elderly people. Have the Disability Alliance a fair point in regarding many elderly people as having significant disabilities which should be recognised by the Social Services or should they expect ageing to take its toll? Write a letter to a local newspaper arguing one point of view.

6 Rank the classes of disabilities in order of their numbers. Calculate each class as a percentage of the total. Now present the data in the form of a pie graph.

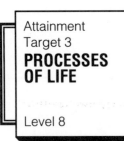

Attainment
Target 3
**PROCESSES
OF LIFE**

Level 8

EXERCISE 14

AIDS

By the end of 1988 about 133 000 cases of AIDS had been reported to the World Health Organisation (WHO). In the UK, by 1989, 1116 people had died from AIDS. There is a larger group of people who do not have full-blown AIDS but are infected by the Human Immunodeficiency Virus (HIV). Estimates suggest that between 20 000 and 50 000 people are infected with HIV in the UK.

Being infected with HIV does not mean that the individual necessarily has AIDS but many researchers believe that all cases will eventually develop into AIDS.

1 What does AIDS stand for?

2 It is not possible to tell by looking at someone whether they are carrying HIV. Carrying HIV does not mean the carrier has AIDS, but it does mean that it can be passed on. Find out how AIDS is spread.

3 In as much detail as you can, explain what the block graph shows about survival and death from AIDS in the UK.

4 The line graphs show what researchers consider to be the worst possible scenario for the future and the most likely scenario. Describe the factors which could lead to each of those outcomes.

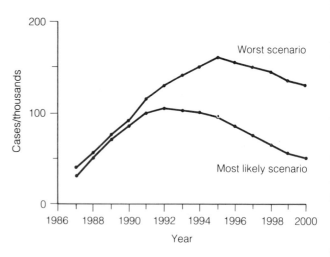

Projected number of HIV positives

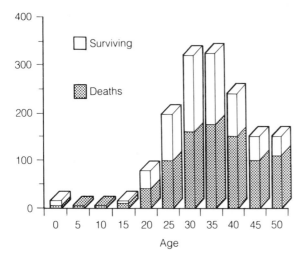

AIDS cases and deaths in the UK

The fight against AIDS in those already suffering from the disease is being fought along three lines:
  (a) reducing the risk of secondary infection
  (b) increasing the response of the individual's immune system
  (c) inhibiting the virus.

All of these require the development of drugs. The most recent to gain public awareness is AZT, but a year's supply of this drug, which inhibits the virus, costs £4700. Patients using this drug have survived, on average, just under a year. Some suggest that the best course is to provide AIDS sufferers with painkillers. This is by far the cheapest method of dealing with the symptoms.

5 How do you think we should fight AIDS? What is your opinion? Write an account which explains what you think. Make sure you cover public education and ignorance, the cost of research and the feelings of the AIDS sufferers themselves.

ESSENTIAL SCIENCE ACTIVITIES © K. Bishop, W. Scott, D. Maddocks, 1990

Attainment
Target 3
**PROCESSES
OF LIFE**

Level 8

EXERCISE 15

Heart Trouble

Many people have heart problems caused by fatty deposits in arteries. These make the artery smaller and can block it completely. This series of drawings shows the technique of angioplasty. It means that blockages in the coronary arteries can be treated without surgery. It works rather like a plumber unblocking drains. A tube (catheter) is inserted in an artery in the groin and is pushed to the heart. Through the tube a balloon is inflated to push the fatty deposits back against the artery wall and to stretch it a little. The balloon and catheter are withdrawn leaving the artery clear for the blood to pass as normal. It may block up again in the future but it is quite possible for the process to be repeated and it is much cheaper than open heart surgery.

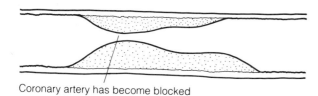

Coronary artery has become blocked

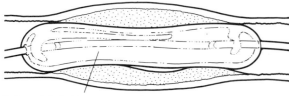

Balloon inflated to open up artery

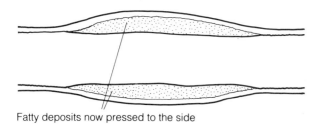

Fatty deposits now pressed to the side

▷ **1** What are the coronary arteries for?

2 The first sign of heart disease is usually angina. Find out what angina is.

3 How could the fatty deposits have built up?

A report from the National Audit Office shows that 180 000 people die each year in the UK from coronary heart disease. This represents a quarter of all deaths in Britain. Other countries, such as Canada, have reduced deaths from heart disease by 40 per cent for men and 50 per cent for women. For the same period in Britain the reductions are 10 per cent for men and only 2 per cent for women. It may be significant that smoking, which is closely associated with heart disease, is actually increasing among teenage girls. The data in the table compare the mortality (death) rates for heart disease across eleven countries.

Country	Deaths from coronary heart disease per 100 000 population	
	Women	Men
Japan	52	45
France	94	130
Finland	265	340
Netherlands	155	235
USA	214	260
Sweden	312	450
England	280	390
Scotland	310	430
Canada	163	230
Australia	191	252
West Germany	210	255

4 Put the figures for each country into rank order starting with the highest first.

5 Draw block graphs to represent the data showing blocks for women and men for each country side by side.

6 Describe any patterns you can see from the graphs and attempt to explain them.

7 Why might Japan have the lowest death rate from coronary heart disease?

Attainment
Target 3
**PROCESSES
OF LIFE**

Level 9

EXERCISE 16

Photosynthesis

Market gardeners are keen to provide the best conditions for their plants to grow as fast as possible. Growth depends on the rate at which the plants photosynthesise.

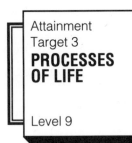

Carbon dioxide taken up

Water taken in

Carbohydrate synthesised

Oxygen released into the atmosphere

Chlorophyll absorbs light energy from the sun

▷ **1** Using a copy of the drawing, rearrange the labels in the boxes around the plant to explain how photosynthesis works. Put in arrows to show where the processes happen.

Researchers into plant growth have investigated the effects of light intensity, CO_2 concentration and temperature. By measuring the rate at which the plants use up CO_2 it is possible to assess how well they are growing.

2 Analyse the graphs carefully and decide which of the following statements are true. Explain why you think the other statements are invalid.
 (a) The rate of photosynthesis always changes with the light intensity.
 (b) The rate of photosynthesis increases in direct proportion with CO_2 concentration.
 (c) The rate of photosynthesis is greater at 30 °C than at 15 °C.
 (d) A temperature of 50 °C would increase the rate of photosynthesis even more.
 (e) Increasing the amount of CO_2 present has more effect than increasing the temperature.

3 The experimental design assumes that the rate of photosynthesis is best measured by recording the rate at which CO_2 is used up by the plant. What is the explanation for this and why do you think it is better than using oxygen production as a measure of photosynthesis?

4 When comparing the growth of plants what other factors must be controlled for the experiments to be fair?

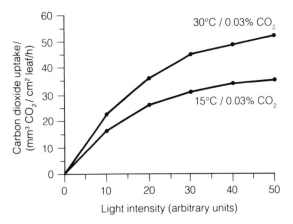

Rate of growth of marrow plants

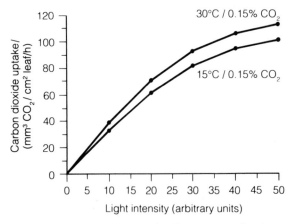

Rate of growth of marrow plants

EXERCISE 17

Abortion

LIFE and the British Pregnancy Advisory Service (BPAS) are two organisations with opposing views about abortion.

> BPAS accepts the possibility of abortion and will offer advice about both abortion and adoption where an unwanted baby is concerned. The advice given depends on the individual case but the emphasis is put on the welfare and the rights of the mother. BPAS will also advocate abortion in cases where tests show that genetic abnormalities, such as spina bifida or cystic fibrosis, are present in the foetus.

> LIFE believes that abortion at any stage of a pregnancy is wrong. It believes that life begins at conception when a sperm fertilises an ovum. Termination of the pregnancy is only accepted if there is a direct risk to the life of the mother. LIFE will offer advice to pregnant women who do not wish to keep their babies encouraging them not to have an abortion but allowing their babies to go for adoption.

▷ The two organisations differ fundamentally about where life begins, about the rights of the unborn child and about the right of the mother to choose whether or not to terminate the pregnancy.

1 Write down the advice you think each organisation would give to mothers who find themselves in the following situations:

(a) genetic screening has shown a woman, 18 weeks into her pregnancy, that her baby is likely to suffer from spina bifida.
(b) a 17-year-old girl, 6 weeks into her pregnancy feels that her personal and social circumstances are such that she could not cope with either her pregnancy or the birth of the baby.
(c) a woman has contracted German measles (Rubella) during the early stages of her pregnancy and has been told that this will increase the chances of her child being seriously damaged at birth.

2 Write down your views on each situation.

3 Explain why girls in their early teens should be immunised against *Rubella*.

4 What is meant by the term 'genetic screening'?

Research

1 Obtain literature from the British Pregnancy Advisory Service and LIFE by writing to them. Look up their addresses in your local telephone book.

2 In a recent debate at the House of Commons MPs decided that the latest time that an abortion may take place will be changed from the 28th week of pregnancy to the 24th week. Try to obtain information about this debate from sources such as BPAS and LIFE, *New Scientist*, *The Indy* and from back copies of daily newspapers (available in central libraries).

Find out:

(a) reasons why the MPs agreed on a change from 28 weeks to 24 weeks
(b) why they did not accept the suggestion that the change should be from 28 to 18 weeks.

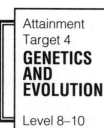

Attainment
Target 4
**GENETICS
AND
EVOLUTION**
Level 8–10

EXERCISE 18

Test-tube Babies

What should you know before your child is born? Should you know gender or be aware of any genetic disorder it might have? Are you then more likely to want an abortion if the child is not the gender you wanted, or if it is likely to be born deformed or with a disability? These questions of medical ethics concern us all. The following technique highlights the problem.

A new in vitro genetic screening technique removes up to about thirty eggs from the mother. On average six of these will be successfully fertilised by in vitro fertilisation (IVF), and produce six test-tube embryos. These will then be screened for genetic disorders and the healthy ones replaced in the mother's uterus. The success rate so far is only nine per cent.

The present law allows this kind of research to be carried out on embryos up to fourteen days old. Beyond that it is not permitted. Many people want to prevent it altogether.

⇨ **1** Do you think this technique is ethical, that is morally right? Argue from two points of view:
   (a) from the point of view of a couple who have had many abortions because of genetic abnormalities
   (b) from the point of view of the person who believes that all life is sacred.

This is a situation familiar to many couples whose families have a history of genetic disorders.

Peter and Sally Miller would like to have children but they are very concerned about a genetic disorder called cystic fibrosis. There is a history of this inherited disorder in both their families. Mr Miller's uncle (Steve Miller) had it and so did a niece of Mrs Miller's mother (Mary Jones). The diagram shows part of their family trees.

2 Make up a possible genetic history for the two families and work out the chances of the Millers having a child with cystic fibrosis.
Use C = the normal gene and
   c = the gene that causes cystic fibrosis.
Assume that the normal gene is dominant and only the presence of a double recessive (cc) will cause the problem.

3 Each of the following are genetic disorders which can be detected by genetic screening.

   (a) sickle cell anaemia
   (b) Down's syndrome
   (c) thalassaemia
   (d) cystic fibrosis
   (e) haemophilia

Below are descriptions of these disorders. Match each disorder with the appropriate description.

(i) Blood lacks a special clotting factor
(ii) Disorder of various glands such as those in the lungs and digestive system
(iii) Problems associated with the manufacture of haemoglobin
(iv) Defect of mental and physical development caused by an extra chromosome
(v) Faulty red blood cells with characteristic shape

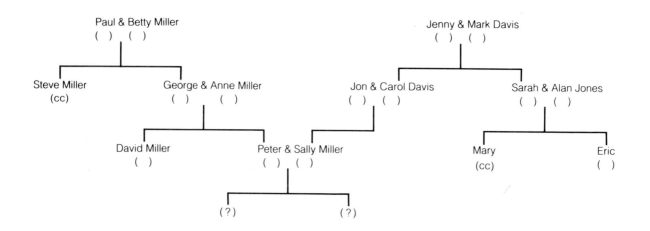

Attainment
Target 4
**GENETICS
AND
EVOLUTION**
Level 8–10

EXERCISE 19

Colour Blind?

Four per cent of human males are colour blind but very few females are. By contrast South American squirrel monkeys are not so lucky. All males are colour blind and so are many of the females.

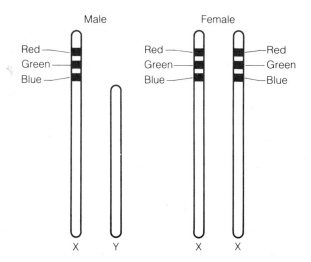

Human chromosomes

Squirrel monkey

The genes for colour vision in both human and squirrel monkeys lie on the X chromosome. In humans the genes for red, green and blue lie at different points along the X chromosome. In squirrel monkeys the red and green genes must 'fight' for the same spot on the X chromosome.

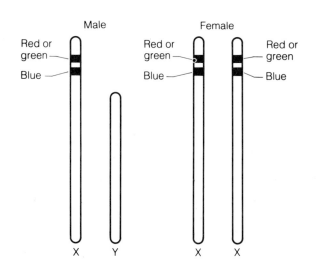

Squirrel monkey chromosomes

☞ **1** Use these diagrams to explain the information about colour blindness in humans and squirrel monkeys presented in the first paragraph.

2 What are the advantages of being able to distinguish between red and green.

At one time all the squirrel monkeys were red-green colour blind, but at some point a mutation occurred which allowed both red and green genes to exist. This gave some of the female monkeys a competitive advantage because then they could tell ripe from unripe fruit clearly and it was much easier to see insects which hide themselves by camouflage.

3 Explain the term 'mutation'.

4 Why does the mutant gene offer no benefit to the male squirrel monkey? Draw a genetic diagram to show why it is impossible for the male to achieve red-green colour vision.

5 What process must occur again for male monkeys to distinguish red-green?

6 This kind of colour blindness is said to be a sex-linked disorder. What is meant by 'sex-linked'?

ESSENTIAL SCIENCE ACTIVITIES   © K. Bishop, W. Scott, D. Maddocks, 1990

Attainment
Target 4
**GENETICS
AND
EVOLUTION**
Level 8–10

EXERCISE 20

Blood Groups

Before a blood transfusion takes place the patient's blood group must be known. Giving the wrong blood could be disastrous. Knowing people's blood groups can also be used for other purposes such as working out paternity, that is discovering who the father of a child is.

The table below gives the four phenotypes in the ABO blood grouping system and the genotypes that give rise to them.

Phenotype (blood group)	Genotype (genetic make-up)
A	AA or AO
B	BB or BO
AB	AB
O	OO

The genes that determine which blood group you are occur in pairs. Genes A and B are both dominant to gene O. However if they occur together they are co-dominant. Gene O is therefore recessive.

Example:
The inheritance of blood groups.

Parents	Mother	Father
Phenotype	A	A
Genotype	AO	AA
Eggs/sperm	A or O	only A
Children	AA	AO

This means that both parents were blood group A. It was known that they had different genotypes. The mother's eggs could carry either the O or the A gene, whereas the father's sperm carried only the A gene. When the father's sperm fertilised an egg the result could be either a genotype combination of AO or AA. In both cases the resulting phenotype of any child is bound to be blood group A because the A gene is dominant to the O gene.

1 If one of the children in the example was discovered to be blood group O, what must the father's genotype have been? Draw a genetic diagram which shows what must have occurred.

2 Complete the genetic diagram below to show what the possible blood groups of the children could be.

Parents	Mother	Father
Phenotype	AB	O
Genotype		
Eggs/sperm		
Children		

Why are none of the children blood group O?

3 Complete the genetic diagram below which gives only the genotypes of the parents.

Parents	Mother	Father
Phenotype		
Genotype	AO	BO
Eggs/sperm		
Children		

Work out the percentage chances of any child born from these parents having a particular blood group.

4 These are the details of a simplified paternity suit.
A married couple both have blood group O. At some point in time the wife has an extra-marital affair after which a child is born. It is not known whether the husband is the father or not. Depending on the child's blood group it is sometimes possible to tell if the father is the husband.
Who do you think the father is if the child is:
(a) group A, (b) group B, (c) group O?
When is it impossible to tell who is the father of the child?

ESSENTIAL SCIENCE ACTIVITIES © K. Bishop, W. Scott, D. Maddocks, 1990

Attainment
Target 5
**HUMAN
INFLUENCES
ON THE EARTH**
Level 9

EXERCISE 21

Global Warming

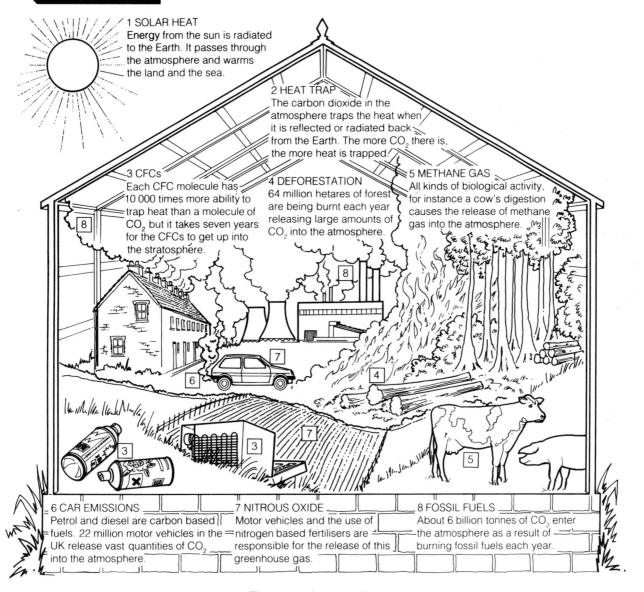

1 SOLAR HEAT
Energy from the sun is radiated to the Earth. It passes through the atmosphere and warms the land and the sea.

2 HEAT TRAP
The carbon dioxide in the atmosphere traps the heat when it is reflected or radiated back from the Earth. The more CO_2 there is, the more heat is trapped.

3 CFCs
Each CFC molecule has 10 000 times more ability to trap heat than a molecule of CO_2 but it takes seven years for the CFCs to get up into the stratosphere.

4 DEFORESTATION
64 million hetares of forest are being burnt each year releasing large amounts of CO_2 into the atmosphere.

5 METHANE GAS
All kinds of biological activity, for instance a cow's digestion causes the release of methane gas into the atmosphere.

6 CAR EMISSIONS
Petrol and diesel are carbon based fuels. 22 million motor vehicles in the UK release vast quantities of CO_2 into the atmosphere.

7 NITROUS OXIDE
Motor vehicles and the use of nitrogen based fertilisers are responsible for the release of this greenhouse gas.

8 FOSSIL FUELS
About 6 billion tonnes of CO_2 enter the atmosphere as a result of burning fossil fuels each year.

The greenhouse effect

The greenhouse effect is a major environmental problem created by humans.

In the last 100 years the Earth has warmed up by more than half a degree Celsius. This does not seem much but small changes in temperature could mean rising sea levels all round the globe. Some scientists believe that a rise of between 20 cm and 1.5 m can be predicted by the year 2030 and cause low-lying areas of the world to return to marsh and swampland.

What can be done?

One solution suggested by BNFL (British Nuclear Fuels Limited) is an increase in the role of nuclear power in a 'balanced energy policy for this country'. Electricity generated by nuclear power does not release CO_2 into the atmosphere. Is this the answer?

▷ Write an article for a newspaper based on one of the following points of view;
  (a) As a representative of BNFL
  (b) As a representative of an environmental group
  (c) As someone who lives close to the nuclear reprocessing plant at Sellafield
  (d) As someone who lives in a lowland area of Britain which could be flooded if the polar ice caps start to melt.

ESSENTIAL SCIENCE ACTIVITIES © K. Bishop, W. Scott, D. Maddocks, 1990

Attainment
Target 5
**HUMAN
INFLUENCES
ON THE EARTH**

Level 9

EXERCISE 22

Pollution of the North Sea

Every year Britain dumps 250 000 tonnes of liquid industrial waste and large quantities of sewage sludge directly into the North Sea. The table shows how the rivers also bring wastes to the North Sea.

West Germany has agreed to reduce the volume of heavy metal and agricultural chemical pollution from the Rhine by fifty per cent in the next seven years. In return they are asking Britain to cease the dumping of sewage sludge. Britain has agreed that the incineration of toxic waste at sea will be ended by 1994 and the volume of toxic materials discharged into the sea will be halved by 1995. However Britain will still continue to dump coal mining waste into the sea off the Durham coast. Although it is an eyesore along the beaches as it is washed up, it is not considered toxic.

⟐ **1** Look at the map of north west Europe and identify the seven countries with North Sea coasts.

2 Use an atlas to identify the major rivers which flow into the North Sea.

3 For each river write a list of the countries it passes through and note how many major towns or industrial areas are sited along it.

4 Rank the rivers in order for each type of pollution and represent the data as a series of block graphs.

5 Explain why the Rhine is near the top of the list in all four kinds of pollution.

6 If Germany has agreed to cut pollution by the Rhine by fifty per cent in the next seven years calculate the overall percentage drop of pollution in the North Sea for each of the four types.

7 Find out which types of industry are responsible for each of the four types of pollution.

8 Why are environmental organisations so concerned at the level of pollution in the North Sea? Which industry is most affected by polluted sea water?

9 Write down alternatives to the dumping of toxic waste and sewage sludge at sea and suggest why they are not being used.

10 Coal waste makes the sea cloudy. Draw a diagram of a typical marine food chain and show how the coal waste interferes with it.

River	Mercury (tonnes pa)	Cadmium (tonnes pa)	Nitrogen (thousand tonnes pa)	Phosphorus (thousand tonnes pa)
Forth	0.1	2.0	1	-
Tyne	1.4	1.3	1	0.2
Tees	0.6	0.6	2	0.2
Humber	0.7	3.5	41	0.6
Thames	1.1	1.5	31	0.1
Scheldt	1.0	7.4	62	7.0
Rhine	3.9	13.8	420	37.0
Ems	0.4	0.7	22	0.7
Weser	1.1	2.9	87	3.8
Elbe	7.3	8.4	150	12.0

RIVER POLUTION OF THE NORTH SEA

North West Europe

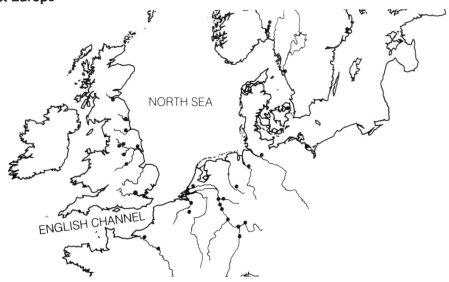

Attainment
Target 5
**HUMAN
INFLUENCES
ON THE EARTH**

Level 10

EXERCISE 23

Stubble Burning

The following letters are part of a debate going on in a newspaper about the effect of farmers who burn the stubble once the straw has been harvested. You might well have seen clouds of black smoke rising up into the sky and wondered what the fire was. Lots of people do not like it simply because it produces clouds of black soot. Others argue that it contributes to the greenhouse effect.

Read the letters and follow the debate.

The first letter (opposite) is a response to a claim made by the National Society for Clean Air (NSCA) which says that the burning of stubble contributes to the greenhouse effect by releasing carbon dioxide.

The next two letters are replies to the first.

Whether stubble is disposed of by burning in the field, incineration, burning for fuel or biodegradation, it will release the same amount of CO_2 into the atmosphere, which will then be absorbed by cereal plants during the production of the next year's crop of straw. This situation would not be changed by any of the proposed uses of straw, such as paper-making, since the products will still be dissipated after a few years.

The greenhouse effect is too serious to warrant using it as an all-purpose bogey in justification of unrelated contentions. It originates in the burning of fossil fuels, which are in excess of the natural carbon cycle on which all life depends, and will only be remedied by reducing the consumption of these fuels.

The fact that the NSCA makes such an inaccurate claim makes me doubt the validity of their other claims that straw burning releases dioxins, carbon monoxide and nitrogen oxides.

Straw is notoriously deficient in nitrogen, which makes it un-suitable, in itself, as a fertiliser, so why should it release appreciable quantities of nitrogen oxides when burnt?

Your correspondent is not correct in claiming that the practice of burning straw, as opposed to allowing it to degrade naturally, does not affect carbon dioxide levels in the air. He has not considered the effect of the differing rates of release of carbon dioxide.

The carbon in straw is not contributing to the greenhouse effect. It will only do so after it is converted to carbon dioxide in the air. Burning the straw ensures that the carbon dioxide is formed immediately, whereas with biodegradation it will take months. Use of the straw for other purposes such as paper-making could leave the carbon outside the atmosphere for years. In terms of the carbon cycle, burning reduces the proportion of carbon bound in organic matter and increases the proportion in the atmospheric part of the cycle. These arguments of course apply to any other organic matter, such as waste timber, autumn leaves and even unwanted plastics.

Allowing biodegradation to take place will also increase populations of the living organisms that decompose the organic matter. Allowing timber to decay naturally has long been recommended as a conservation measure. The same reasoning applies to straw, although the organisms that benefit are not usually as large or visible as those found on rotting timber. As regards the possibility of burning releasing pollutants, it is known that toxic compounds are produced by burning some organic compounds, both synthetic and natural. Further, any inefficient burning – where the supply of oxygen cannot keep up with the rate of burning – releases some carbon monoxide, and usually also that well known pollutant and known carcinogen, smoke. Yellow flames and smoke are a good indicator of inefficient burning.

* * *

Your correspondent over-simplifies what was, already, only a summary of a report by the NSCA. Fields of burning stubble emit, amongst other gases, carbon monoxide, carbon dioxide, nitrous oxide and nitric oxide without contributing any useful heat that could otherwise be obtained if the straw were to be burned in a furnace. Carbon dioxide and nitrous oxide are contributing to the greenhouse effect, while nitric oxide is thought to have an effect on the ozone in the atmosphere. Nitrogen oxides add to the effect of sulphur dioxide in acid rain by forming nitric and nitrous acids.

Fields sprayed with nitrogen fertilisers give off nitrogen oxides for a few days. Soil bacteria feed off the fertilisers and themselves make these gases. Fields of burnt stubble carry on generating nitrogen oxides for at least six months. The bacteria feed on the rich supply of ammonia left behind from the firing, which lasts for months. The nitrogen comes not so much from the straw but from the air. In a nutshell, the burning of straw is creating long-lasting dangers and pollutes the atmosphere for months afterwards.

▷ **1** After having read the three letters do you think straw burning does contribute to the greenhouse effect or not? Use evidence from the letters to support your view.

2 The first letter suggests it is unlikely that straw burning releases oxides of nitrogen. The second letter says it is possible. By what process?

3 The third correspondent says that the yellow flames you see indicate inefficient burning. What are the consequences of this?

4 Find out why farmers wish to burn the stubble and are not pleased at it being banned in 1992.

Attainment
Target 5
**HUMAN
INFLUENCES
ON THE EARTH**
Level 6

EXERCISE 24

Maps of the World

The maps on this page show two quite different projections of the land mass of the Earth. The first is Mercator's projection and the second is Peter's projection. Look at the maps carefully and answer the questions below.

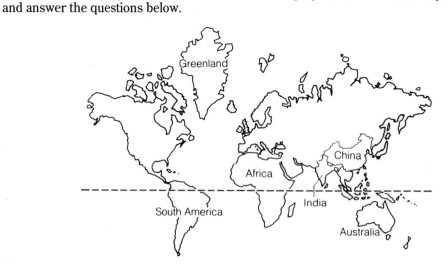

Mercator's map

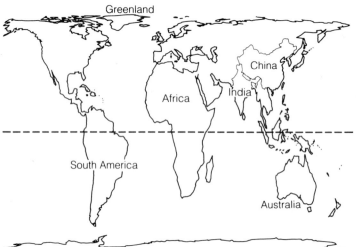

Peter's map

1 The equator is marked on both maps. What do you notice about the amount of land north and south of the equator on the two maps? What are the other main differences between the maps?

2 Look at the position of Europe on both maps. Why do you think it was given such a central position on the early maps?

3 The Peter's map has all the different parts of the Earth (land and oceans) in proportion. That is one square centimetre on the map represents an equal area of the Earth's surface – no matter where on the Earth it is. This is not the case with the Mercator map.

On a sheet of clear acetate or tracing paper mark out a 0.5 cm square grid (4 cm x 4 cm). Put this over the maps and estimate on each map the surface areas of: Greenland, Africa, China, South America, Australia and India.

Present your data like this :

Landmass	Number of squares area on	
	Mercator map	Peter's map
Greenland		

4 It has been said of the new Peter's map that 'it challenges our established ways of looking at the world – in particular the way we view the "Third World"'. What do you think this means?

Attainment
Target 5
**HUMAN
INFLUENCES
ON THE EARTH**

Level 8

EXERCISE 25

Going, Going...

Fires of devastation

If the destruction of the Amazon forests goes on at the present rate they will be gone within the next thirty years.

Approximately 200 000 square kilometres of Amazon forest are cut and burnt every year; of these 80 000 are actually virgin forest. But why should it worry us in the developed world? There are several reasons why.

Trees contain a large amount of carbon. If they are burnt they release carbon dioxide into the atmosphere, and this is one of the gases responsible for global warming – the greenhouse effect. Ten years ago it was estimated that forest burning throughout the world released two billion tons of carbon dioxide, whereas fossil fuel burning released about five billion tons of carbon dioxide each year. The difference since then is that fossil fuel burning has remained relatively constant, but forest burning is increasing dramatically.

The irony of this process is that the very thing which is ideal for mopping up excess carbon dioxide in the atmosphere is itself being burnt, releasing massive amounts of carbon dioxide. Not only that, the forest is also a kind of global lung because as it soaks up carbon dioxide it releases oxygen.

As the Amazon rainforests burn, species of plants, insects, mammals, reptiles and birds are thought to be disappearing at a rate approaching a hundred a day. Going is a massive resource – the forests offer biodiversity. Apart from the sheer tragedy a reservoir of untapped organisms is going without us having any idea what they can provide in medical or agricultural terms.

The rainforests are rich, but strangely the soils in which they stand are impoverished. Once cut down they expose a soil which can only support the cultivation of crops for a year or two before it is blown or washed away. How can this be? The reason is that the trees themselves hold nearly all the nutrients, with the soil below acting as a sort of recycling agent. The soil holds almost nothing.

Mahogany and teak are probably the two best known hardwoods. Polished up they look magnificent. But of course they are a natural part of the rainforest cut down and exported to richer countries elsewhere.

The smell of charcoal burning in the forest is another sad reminder of the destruction. Close by the charcoal ovens are the smelters used to produce a very poor steel. This is an example of a high-grade resource being used to produce a low-grade product. Clearing the forest also makes room for cash crops. Coffee growing is a major industry in the Amazon.

Sadly too, man inflicts the punishment on his own kind. The native Amazonian Indians are being driven from the rainforests as the gold-diggers pursue the riches, the cattle farmers graze their herds to make beefburgers and the technologists pursue the energy harnessed in the river systems. And all the time the one sustainable resource is being squandered, never to be replaced.

Where does the fault lie? Why is there this desperate rush to denude the world of its biological heritage?

Certainly the fault does not lie with the local populations alone. Given present economic conditions many of the countries are up to their eyes in debt, and so the clearance of the rainforest to exploit mineral resources or develop cheaper supplies of energy or cultivate cash crops is all too understandable. The question is how can we stop it?

This is an article written by the environmental correspondent of a newspaper. It mixes scientific fact with emotional or sensational phrases beginning with the banner headline. *Read the article and answer the following questions.*

➭ **1** The rainforest is described as the planet's global lung. Explain this in terms of photosynthesis.

2 Some scientists say that the rainforest cannot soak up atmospheric CO_2 because it is already a stable climax community. Explain what you think they mean.

3 Explain the reasons for soil erosion once the rainforest has been cleared.

4 The article uses the term biodiversity. Find out what this word means and explain the point being made.

5 Draw a flow diagram to show what might happen to the ecology of the world as deforestation continues.

6 The article is written by a journalist rather than an academic scientist. Find three phrases from the article which indicate this and explain why they might have been used.

Attainment
Target 6

TYPES AND
USES OF
MATERIALS

Level 10

EXERCISE 26

Metal Resources

This is a map of the world using Peter's projection. It is a new way of looking at countries. With this map you can compare the size of one country with another. If they are the same size on the map, they are the same size on the ground.

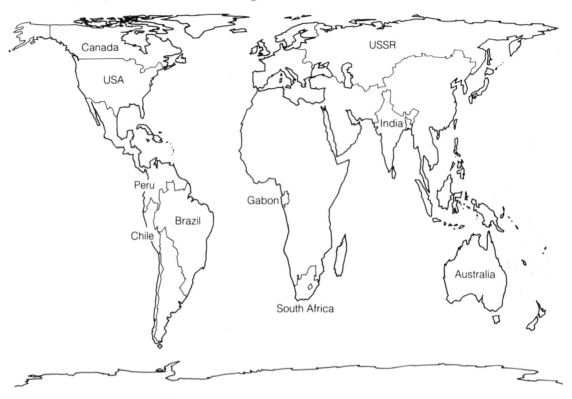

Map of the world – Peter's projection

▷ **1** Does anything surprise you about the map?

2 Study the table of figures about the world's metal resources.

Your task is to devise a way of putting information about resource production, shown in the table, onto the map, so that it is clear. You will need to provide a key to the map to make it easy to understand by anyone trying to use it.

In your group think about and talk about the ways of putting this information onto the map. Remember that you have to distinguish between the resources in a clear way. Are you going to put numbers on the map or represent the figures in some way by a shape, for example a bar graph? Discuss your ideas with your teacher before you start.

3 Is there any evidence in the data to support this statement? 'The distribution of the production of lead and zinc in the Earth is different from that of copper and manganese.' Write down your reasons.

4 The ores to produce three of these resources were widely mined in the UK last century. Find out where the mining areas were. Why do you think mining is no longer carried out?

Country	Resource production (thousands of tonnes per year)			
	Lead	Copper	Manganese	Zinc
Australia	400	—	760	480
Brazil	—	—	1270	—
Canada	260	730	—	980
Chile	—	1010	—	—
Gabon	—	—	1090	—
India	—	—	670	—
Peru	180	—	2990	460
South Africa	—	—	2410	—
USA	550	1460	—	420
USSR	470	1130	—	718
Total world production	3330	8000	9840	5520

ESSENTIAL SCIENCE ACTIVITIES   © K. Bishop, W. Scott, D. Maddocks, 1990

Attainment
Target 6

**TYPES AND
USES OF
MATERIALS**

Level 5

EXERCISE 27

Discovering Resources

Read the following passage about the discovery and exploitation of resources in two imaginary countries. Then answer the questions that follow.

Sursia is the only producer of the strategic resource **Hafnalum**. Cameria is the only importer. By the year 2005 the known reserves of Hafnalum were 500 000 tonnes but there was an unused stockpile in Cameria of 100 000 tonnes. Cameria was importing Hafnalum at a rate of 25 000 tonnes a year even though only 20 000 tonnes a year were being used.

This rate of usage lasted for 5 years until 2010. Then, in 2011, the new rulers of Sursia decided to limit their exports to 15 000 tonnes a year. Five years later, in 2016, this was cut again to 10 000 tonnes a year. During this period the rate of use of Hafnalum by Cameria remained constant.

In 2015, however, Cameria had realised that it would run out of Hafnalum in the early 2020s. Its scientists began working on methods of recycling used Hafnalum to increase Cameria's supply. The method was perfected in 2021 and from that year on an extra 5000 tonnes of Hafnalum were available to Cameria.

In 2031, Camerian scientists invented a way of using Hafnalum so that only 5 000 tonnes a year were needed, but found that 10% of the material had to be newly produced and not recycled. Cameria continued to import Hafnalum at a rate of 10 000 tonnes a year.

In 2036, the Sursian government announced that in 2040 they would stop exporting Hafnalum.

1 On one set of axes labelled mass and time plot graphs (using different colours) of:
   (a) Sursian reserves of Hafnalum
   (b) the Camerian stockpile of Hafnalum
   (c) the rate of usage of Hafnalum by Cameria.

2 Use the graphs to answer these questions:
   (a) At the end of 2030 how long could Cameria have gone on using Hafnalum at the rate of 20 000 tonnes a year?
   (b) Recycling was introduced in the year 2021. Using the recycled Hafnalum, how many years use did Cameria still have?

(c) In 2030, what were:
   (i) the Sursian reserves of Hafnalum?
   (ii) the Camerian stockpile?
(d) At the new rate of usage introduced in 2031, how long could Cameria continue to use Hafnalum?

3 Sketch on the graph how you think the price of Hafnalum changed from 2005 to 2039. (You will need to make your own scale on the *y*-axis).

4 If you were President of Cameria in 2039, what would you do?

Attainment
Target 7

**MAKING NEW
MATERIALS**

Level 9

EXERCISE 28

Polymers

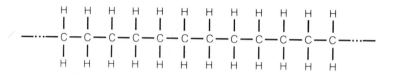

Structure I

Structure II

There are about 25
side chains per 100
carbon atoms.

Side chains

Plastics are important in our lives today. There are about twenty which we use regularly.

Polythene is a plastic. It is a polymer of ethene, from which it gets its name. It is manufactured in two forms: high density (HD) and low density (LD) polythene. The molecular structure of the two types is shown above.

Here are some properties of the two types of polythene:

Property	LD	HD
Density (g cm^{-3})	0.92	0.96
Tensile strength (N m^{-2})	1×10^7	3×10^7
Percentage stretch before breaking	400%	200%

Use the data and structures shown to answer the questions.

▷ **1** Which polymer:
(a) will stretch the farther?
(b) is the stronger?
(c) occupies the most space when 1 kg of one polythene is compared with 1 kg of the other?

2 Which of the two structures represents HD polythene, and which LD polythene? Give reasons for your answer. (Hint: think of the chains being laid alongside each other in the closest possible way.)

3 Explain why structure II is not a realistic picture of the actual molecule.

4 What is the difference in mass between a 1 m³ block of LD polythene and a 1 m³ block of HD polythene?

Attainment
Target 7

**MAKING NEW
MATERIALS**

Level 9

EXERCISE 29

Rubber

We use polymers every day. Some we eat – starch in rice and potatoes. Some we wear – cotton underwear, nylon anoraks. Some we sit on – polyurethane foam. Some we ride on – rubber tyres.

Every year billions of new rubber tyres are manufactured and just as many wear out. What happens to these tyres? Are they biodegradable? Can they be re-cycled? Do some research and find out what garages do with worn out tyres.

The rubber we use today comes from both natural and synthetic sources. Rubber is a giant molecule, or polymer, made up of millions of tiny repeating units. Another polymer with the same repeating unit is gutta-percha.

Rubber and gutta-percha have quite different properties yet both have the same chemical formula. The reason for this is that the arrangement of the repeating unit in the polymer is different.

Tyre dump

Structure I

Structure II

▷ **1** The structures of rubber and gutta-percha are shown above but with their middle sections missing. Draw each structure and complete the middle sections.

2 Polymers are formed by the reaction of small molecules known as monomers. In the polypropylene molecule shown below the repeating unit is ringed. Look at the structure of rubber and gutta-percha and write down the repeating structure in each of them.

3 Rubber and gutta-percha are addition polymers: monomers are added to one another in a chain. Work out the structure of the monomer from which they are both made.

4 Gutta-percha , although similar to rubber in some ways, is a tough solid, which was once used as the outer cover of golf balls. Given these different properties, say which of the structures, I or II, is rubber and which is gutta-percha. Give a simple explanation of your reasons.

5 Rubber has many uses in industry and the home. Write down as many of them as you can.

6 Find out if gutta-percha has any uses today.

ESSENTIAL SCIENCE ACTIVITIES   © K. Bishop, W. Scott, D. Maddocks, 1990

Attainment
Target 7

**MAKING NEW
MATERIALS**

Level 9

EXERCISE 30

Bonding

Many compounds are held together by covalent chemical bonds. These bonds are usually shown as straight lines between the symbols of the atoms. Double lines are used to show double bonds and triple lines for triple bonds.

For example, carbon dioxide is shown as:

O = C = O

There are some simple rules which must always be obeyed when drawing these diagrams:

hydrogen (H)   atoms have only one bond

oxygen   (O)   atoms have two bonds

nitrogen (N)   atoms have three bonds

carbon   (C)   atoms have four bonds

▷ **1** Follow these rules and draw the bonds on the following structures.

H   H

H   C   C   H

H   H

Ethane (C_2H_6)

H   H

C   C

H   H

Ethene (C_2H_4)

O   O

Oxygen (O_2)

N   N

Nitrogen (N_2)

H   C   C   H

Ethyne (C_2H_2)

H   O   O   H

Hydrogen peroxide (H_2O_2)

H   H   H

H   C   C   C   H

H   H   H

Propane (C_3H_8)

H   H

H   C   N

H   H

Methylamine (CH_3NH_2)

H   H

H   C   C   O   H

H   H

Ethanol (C_2H_5OH)

2 Here are the molecular formulae of six compounds. Draw their structures and put in all the missing bonds.

Butane C_4H_{10}

Propene C_3H_6

Ethanal CH_3CHO

Ethanoic acid CH_3COOH

Glycine CH_2COOH
$\quad\quad\quad\quad\;\; |$
$\quad\quad\quad\quad NH_2$

Alanine $CH_3CHCOOH$
$\quad\quad\quad\quad\quad\; |$
$\quad\quad\quad\quad\quad NH_2$

Attainment
Target 8
**EXPLAINING
HOW
MATERIALS
BEHAVE**
Level 9

EXERCISE 31

Half-life

After the Chernobyl accident sheep farmers in the uplands of North Wales, Scotland and the Lake District were constantly asking the Government how long it would be before the grass would be safe for the sheep to graze on again. But why should it be so long before the grass was safe once more? The answer depends on the type of radioisotopes which had been carried over with the weather and deposited on British soil. Caesium-131 and iodine-133 are typical products of the Chernobyl accident and have half-lives in the order of thirty years and eight days respectively.

Every radioisotope has a half-life. This is the time taken for the mass of an isotope to be halved, e.g. from 100g to 50g. It doesn't matter how much of the isotope you have, the time taken for the mass to be reduced by half will be the same.

Each radioactive isotope has a different half-life. The longer the half-life, the longer the problem of contamination persists.

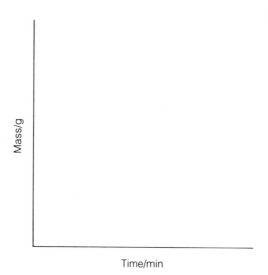

⇨ **1** Three radioisotopes A, B, and C each have different half-lives:
A = 3 minutes
B = 2 minutes
C = 1 minute

Different masses of the pure isotopes are taken and their decay is followed.
A = 120 g
B = 160 g
C = 180 g

Draw three graphs on the same pair of axes to show how the mass of each isotope changes with time (see diagram). Use your graphs to answer questions 2 to 5.

2 At what time after the start are the masses of:
(a) A and B equal?
(b) B and C equal?
(c) A and C equal?

3 When the mass of B drops to 10 g what is the total mass of A, B and C?

4 Which is the first isotope whose mass falls below 1 g?

5 How long will it be before the mass of each of the other two isotopes falls below 1 g?

6 People living in areas where fallout from Chernobyl was likely were advised to take iodine tablets. It seems that the human body preferentially uses iodine-133 rather than normal iodine. Find out why the human body needs iodine and the medical reasons for taking the tablets.

7 A knowledge of half-lives is important in other ways. One of these is the dating of archaeological discoveries. The half-life of the isotope carbon-14 is used by archaeologists. All carbon-containing compounds such as wood, contain a small amount of carbon-14. While a tree is living the proportion of carbon-14 remains the same. When the tree is felled the proportion begins to fall. The half-life of carbon-14 is about 5600 years.
A wooden cross, discovered near Frosterley, is found to have one third of the amount of carbon-14 that it had when the tree was living. Estimate how old the cross is.

8 Why do you think the proportion of carbon-14 in a tree only begins to fall when the tree is killed?

Attainment
Target 8
**EXPLAINING
HOW
MATERIALS
BEHAVE**
Level 8

EXERCISE 32

Isotopes

If you look at a table of atomic mass such as the one given here, none of the values is a whole number.

Element	Average mass number
aluminium	26.98
calcium	40.08
hydrogen	1.01
iron	55.85
mercury	200.60
oxygen	15.99
sodium	22.98
zinc	65.37

This seems surprising if you consider that an atom can only have whole numbers of protons and neutrons. The reason is that every element is made up of a number of different isotopes.

This is best explained by an example.

Copper is made of two main isotopes:

Isotope of copper	Number of protons	Number of neutrons	Percentage found in natural copper
63	29	34	69
65	29	36	31

This means that in every piece of pure copper 69 atoms out of every 100 are isotope-63, and 31 atoms are isotope-65.

⇨ **1** From the table of data how do know that the two isotopes are both copper? What is the only difference between the two isotopes?

2 To calculate the average mass number of copper follow these steps:

(a) assume there are 100 atoms
(b) work out the contribution of each isotope to the average mass;

$$(69 \times 63) + (31 \times 65) =$$

(c) divide by 100 to find the average.

3 Magnesium metal has three isotopes: magnesium-24, magnesium-25 and one other.

The average mass number of pure magnesium is 24.3.

The percentage composition of the three isotopes in pure magnesium is:

magnesium-24	79%
magnesium-25	10%
magnesium-N	11%

Work out the mass number of the other isotope of magnesium. Begin by working out the contribution of each isotope to the average mass number in the following way:

$$(\% \ Mg^{24} \times 24) + (\% \ Mg^{25} \times 25) + (\% \ Mg^{N} x \ N)$$

Add these together and divide by 100 to find out the average mass number. This equals 24.3. From this you can work out the value of N.

4 Why must your answer for N be a whole number?

ESSENTIAL SCIENCE ACTIVITIES   © K. Bishop, W. Scott, D. Maddocks, 1990

Sweating

Remember that cold feeling when the doctor dabs a piece of cotton wool soaked in a liquid on your skin just before you have an injection. This is done to clean the skin and so that you do not feel the needle pierce your skin. The cold feeling is caused by the liquid taking heat from your skin and evaporating into the air. And this is just how sweating works to keep us cool. As sweat evaporates it takes with it heat which it gets from the blood flowing near the surface of the skin. That cool feeling on a hot dry day is even better when there is a nice breeze because the sweat evaporates quickly. But what if there is very little wind and the air is humid. How do you feel then? Usually hot and sticky, but why? The difference depends on the amount of water being carried in the air. If there is already lots in the air then it will not be easy for sweat to evaporate. In fact it stays on your skin and makes you feel sticky.

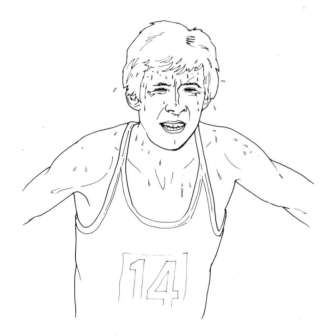

This table shows the maximum amount of water vapour the air can hold at different temperatures.

Temperature(°C)	Mass of water in the air (g m⁻³)
−20	1
−10	2
0	5
10	9
20	18
30	31

▷ **1** Plot a graph using the figures, with the mass of water on the vertical axis and temperature on the horizontal axis. Draw a smooth curve through the points.

Draw your graph so that you can estimate the mass of water vapour that the air would hold at 40 °C. How much is this?

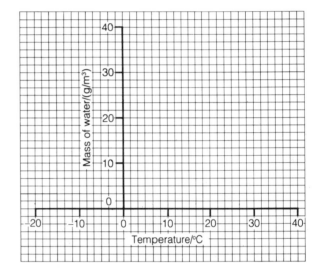

2 From your graph calculate the amount of water that would be released from 1000 m³ of air if the temperature fell from:
(a) 30 °C to 25 °C
(b) 15 °C to 10 °C
(c) 0 °C to −5 °C

3 Describe, in a sentence, the relationship between the temperature of the air and the mass of water it can hold.

4 When saturated air rises by convection it cools rapidly, clouds form, and water falls as rain. Explain why the rainfall in the tropics is often much heavier than it is in the British Isles.

5 The amount of water in the air affects the ability we have to lose heat by sweating. Suggest other ways we can lose heat or help the sweating process.

6 Thinking of the difference between cotton and nylon, why is cotton more comfortable to wear than nylon in humid weather?

Attainment
Target 8
**EXPLAINING
HOW
MATERIALS
BEHAVE**
Level 9

EXERCISE 34

Food Irradiation

The irradiation of food has been banned in the UK since 1967 but it is permitted in 30 countries in the world. A report from the Government's Advisory Committee on Irradiated and Novel Foods claimed there were no special problems with the safety or wholesomeness of irradiated foods, but the British Medical Association (BMA) says that 'food irradiation is another way of covering up manufacturing failures rather than cleaning up the food production chain'.

Opinion polls show that 85–90% of consumers object to food irradiation.

Read the information about irradiation and study the arguments for and against it.

Radiation

The unit used to measure the irradiation of food is the Gray (Gy). It is a measure of the amount of energy given to material by the radiation. 1 Gy is equivalent to 1 joule per kilogram. 1 kilogray (kGy) is 100 Gy.

The amount of energy needed to irradiate food depends on the foodstuff, and on what the purpose of the irradiation is:
• about 1 kGy will be needed to slow down the ripening of fruit or the sprouting of vegetables
• up to 10 kGy will be needed to kill food spoilage bacteria in fish or meat.

Food receives a dose of ionising radiation from a radioactive source such as cobalt-60. By exciting electrons in the molecular structure of the food chemically active ions are formed which start up chemical reactions. Microbes in the food receive the same treatment and many of them are then destroyed in the process.

Arguments for:

• Irradiation keeps food fresh and wholesome longer.

• It significantly reduces the microbial load of the foodstuff thereby reducing the likelihood of microbes causing food poisoning.

• Nutritional losses as a result of irradiation are no more than would occur in normal storage or cooking.

• Irradiation increases the shelf-life of food. Irradiation can be used to delay the ripening of fruit and the sprouting of vegetables. Foods can then be sold to the consumer in far better condition and when they are at their best.

• Irradiation can stop insect pests from breeding and it can kill them.

• Irradiation does not make food radioactive although it does produce chemical changes.

• Irradiated foods will only form a small proportion of any individual's diet.

Arguments against:

• Irradiation damages the nutritional content of food. It destroys some vitamins, particularly B12 and folic acid, in addition to the loss expected from cooking and storage. Some essential polyunsaturated fatty acids are affected.

• No adequate test exists to discover whether food has been irradiated.

• Misuse of the process could increase the number of cases of food poisoning because irradiation can be used to clean up contaminated food and pass it off as wholesome.

• Irradiation does not kill all harmful bacteria. Neither does it destroy toxins already produced by the bacteria.

• Gamma radiation, poorly controlled, could cause the bacteria to mutate and be even more pathogenic than before.

• Irradiation can cause unpleasant flavour changes in oily foods such as fish, fatty meat and cocoa beans. Additives will need to be employed to mask the off-flavours.

• Evidence suggests that stored irradiated wheat fed to animals can produce a genetic disorder called polyploidy, and this in turn can lead to tumours and cancer.

▷ 1 Respond to these issues about food irradiation:
(a) Is it beneficial or harmful?
(b) Can it be detected?
(c) Is it needed?

2 Where do the arguments for and against seem to conflict?

EXERCISE 35

Sunshine Recording

Sunshine recorders are used to produce accurate records of exactly when the sun shines on any particular day. They are used by the meteorological offices as part of their weather recording. The sun's rays are focussed onto a piece of special card and as the sun passes across the sky, it chars a mark onto the card.

Sunshine recording card

⇨ **1** Use the sunshine record shown to work out:
  (a) the times when the sun shone
  (b) the total length of sunshine
  (c) any information you can gather on how strongly the sun was shining.

2 During which season of the year do you think this record was made? What clues did you use to work it out.

3 Some cards that are used are not curved like the one shown. They are straight and are used at

the spring and autumn equinoxes. Explain why a straight card is better.

4 There are two kinds of recorder – one for use near the equator and one for use in higher latitudes. Why do you think two kinds are needed and how will they differ?

5 The four bar graphs show the average sunshine hours and temperatures in Nice in the south of France and in Mexico City. Decide which graphs belong to which countries and explain your reasons for each decision.

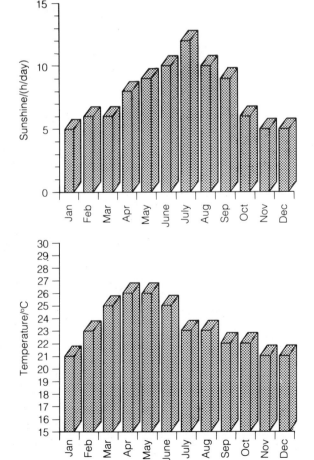

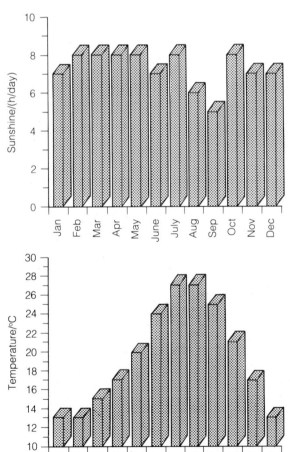

ESSENTIAL SCIENCE ACTIVITIES © K. Bishop, W. Scott, D. Maddocks, 1990

Accident Recoil

AT 7·15 THIS MORNING AN ACCIDENT CLOSED THE CLOCKWISE CARRIAGEWAY OF THE M25 AT JUNCTION 21 JUST BELOW THE M1 INTER-SECTION. A TRUCK RAN INTO THE BACK OF A STATIONARY CAR ON THE HARD SHOULDER. FORTUNATELY THERE WERE NO DEATHS BUT TWO PEOPLE ARE IN HOSPITAL SUFFERING WITH SERIOUS NECK INJURIES. AVOID THE AREA FOR AT LEAST THE NEXT 2 HOURS.

Why is it that when you ask some people, 'Which will stop the quickest, an empty car with just the driver, or a car fully laden with four people?', they say the fully laden car will stop first because it's heavier? Surely common sense will tell you that is wrong. But what is the connection between this and the traffic warning?

The cartoon shows a truck running into the rear of a car. The car is stationary, but when the truck hits it, the car and truck lock together and move forward. From a scientist's point of view this is an example of an inelastic collision.

Just before impact the truck has a certain momentum:

momentum before collision	=	mass of truck (m_1)	×	velocity (v_1)

Just after the collision the truck and car have a combined momentum:

momentum after collision	=	mass of truck + car (m_2)	×	velocity of both (v_2)

The momentum just before the collision equals the momentum just after it:

$$\text{therefore } m_1 \times v_1 = m_2 \times v_2$$

The units for momentum are kg m/s. Mass is therefore measured in kg and velocity in m/s.

▷ **1** A truck had a mass of 10 000 kg and was travelling at 40 mph when it crashed into the back of a stationary car. Use the conversion graph to find the truck's velocity in metres per second.

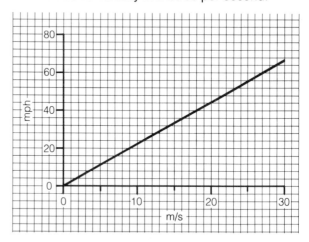

Conversion graph of mph to m/s

2 The car and two passengers have a mass of 1200 kg. Work out the velocity the truck and car have just after the impact.

3 This velocity will quickly fall to zero. Why is this?

4 What is the difference between velocity and speed?

5 Explain why the passengers had neck injuries. What were obviously not fitted in the car?

6 Some cars have impact absorbing bumpers and body work which is designed to crumple. Explain how this reduces the force experienced by the car as the truck hits it.

7 Unladen, the truck has a mass of only 6000 kg. Work out the velocity the car and empty truck would then have immediately after impact.

8 Now use the idea of momentum to explain why people are wrong to think that a fully laden car will take less time to stop than an identical car with just the driver inside.

Stopping

SCREEECH....

The highway code gives the following figures for stopping a car in good conditions:

Speed (mph)	30	40	50	60	70
Thinking distance (ft)	30	40	50	60	70
Braking distance (ft)	45	80	125	180	245
Overall stopping distance (ft)	75	120	175	240	315

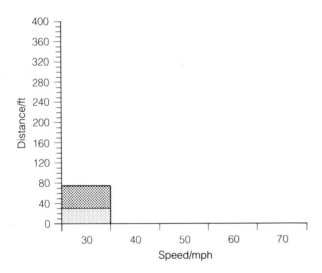

Stopping distances in good driving conditions

➪ **1** Draw a stacked block graph like the one already started, to show the stopping distance data.

2 Work out the mathematical pattern that links the thinking distances and braking distances.

3 Use the graph to work out what the set of figures would be for 20 mph.

4 These figures would be of no use on the continent as the metric system is used there. 100 kph is about the same as 60 mph. Use the patterns in the Highway Code table to complete a table of figures for continental drivers. It has been started for you.

Speed (kph)	20	40	60	80	100	120
Thinking distance (m) Braking distance (m)			12 24			
Overall stopping distance (m)			36			

5 The overall stopping distance is made up of two parts, thinking distance and braking distance. If the braking distance is the distance the car travels from the point the driver's foot hits the brake pedal to the point when the car actually stops, what is the thinking distance?

6 Formula racing cars use different types of tyres according to the track conditions. When it is dry they use 'slicks', which have no tread. When it is wet they use tyres with tread. What is the reason for this?

7 The overall stopping distance depends on lots of factors. Some of these are listed in the table below. Complete the table by putting a tick in those boxes where you think the factor affects the thinking and braking distances.

Factor	Thinking distance		Braking distance	
	increase	decrease	increase	decrease
alcohol				
fit driver				
tired driver				
worn brakes				
wet road				
dry road				
oily road				
poor visibilty				

Attainment
Target 11
**ELECTRICITY
AND
MAGNETISM**
Level 8–9

EXERCISE 38

Power Generation

When electricity is generated and consumed, energy is converted to different forms. For example, it might begin as nuclear energy in uranium and end up as microwave energy in an oven. In all such conversions energy is lost and the process is often very inefficient.

Think about coal being used to generate electricity which then drives a grinding machine in a cement works. The boxes shown here represent each stage in the energy conversions. In each case the top half represents the source of the energy and the bottom half represents the form of the energy. For example:

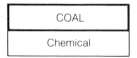

COAL
Chemical

☛ **1** Cut out the boxes and stick them down the left hand side of a page in the correct order, beginning with coal.

2 Complete each box showing the source, *and* the form of the energy.

3 Write alongside each box any of the ways that energy could be lost at that stage. These might include heat, sound, vibration, etc.

4 In some energy transfers the loss of energy is quite high. Use the figures below to calculate how much grinding energy is obtained from 1000 units of chemical energy in the coal.

Process	Percentage energy loss
Generating electricity from coal	70
Transmission of electricity	10
Transforming electricity	2
Electric grinding energy	20

5 Write down any other ways that you can think of to reduce energy loss at each step.

6 Are there any ways the energy could be used more efficiently?

7 Now make up your own flow chart beginning with water in a cloud falling on a reservoir in a hydroelectric power scheme, and ending with light in a fluorescent tube.

COAL		FURNACE		MOTOR IN GRINDER

GRINDING MECHANISM		TRANSFORMER		BOILER

POWER LINES		GENERATOR		TRANSFORMER

Attainment
Target 11
**ELECTRICITY
AND
MAGNETISM**
Level 6

EXERCISE 39

The Right Fuse

Fitting the wrong fuse in the plug which connects an appliance to the mains is a common fault. If you go to a supermarket and buy plugs they are nearly all fitted with 13 amp fuses. That is fine for an appliance such as a heater or a kettle which draws a lot of electric current, but it will not protect a cassette player or a small hair drier. You need to know how to work out which fuse to fit: generally this is a 3 amp, 5 amp or 13 amp fuse.

To work out the correct fuse, you need to look at the information given on the appliance. It usually looks like this.

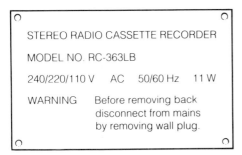

The voltage of a domestic mains supply is 240 V in the UK. In order to find out the current drawn by the appliance you also need to know the wattage (or power rating). In this case you can see it is 11 W.

We can use this pattern to work out the current drawn.

$$\text{Current drawn} = \frac{\text{watts}}{\text{volts}}$$

$$\text{Current drawn} = \frac{11 \text{ W}}{240 \text{ V}}$$

$$= 0.05 \text{ A}$$

As this is less than 3 amps then a fuse no greater than 3 amps should be fitted.

➪ **1** Work out the correct size of fuse needed to protect the following appliances in a 240 V circuit:
 (a) 100 W lamp
 (b) 250 W towel rail
 (c) 2 kW heater.

2 How many 3 kW heaters would work at full power on a 30 amp ring main circuit?

3 Here are instructions about what to do when you suspect that a fuse has blown in a plug. At the moment they are in the wrong order. Rearrange them in a sensible order and see if you agree with other people in your group.
 (a) Screw the plug cover back on.
 (b) Remove the plug from the socket.
 (c) Check the plug to make sure all the wires are firmly in place.
 (d) Insert a fuse of the correct size.
 (e) Switch off the appliance.
 (f) Remove the fuse.
 (g) Check the appliance is now working.
 (h) Switch off at the wall socket.
 (i) Check that the flex grip is properly tightened.
 (j) Unscrew the top cover of the plug.

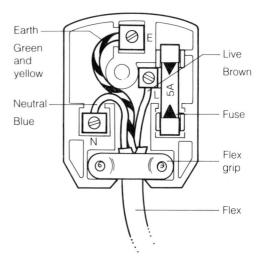

4 It has been suggested that plugs should be sold without a fuse so that the correct fuse can be fitted afterwards. Summarise the arguments for and against this idea.

Attainment
Target 11
**ELECTRICITY
AND
MAGNETISM**
Level 6

EXERCISE 40

Electricity Bills

The Johnson family live in a large flat above a shop which has just been converted to a laundrette. They received an electricity bill in October for the third quarter demanding a staggering £703. 36. They knew it could not be right. The first thing they did was check the meter. It read 365 432 Units. The previous reading was 352 839 Units, a difference of 12 593 Units. At 6 pence per unit this would give a sum of the order the Electricity Board were claiming they owed. The Board said they found nothing wrong with the meter when they checked it.

Mrs. Johnson had filed all the bills since they moved into the flat 5 years ago. She tabulated the units for each quarter:

Year	Jan-Mar	Apr-Jun	Jul-Sep	Oct-Dec
1985	2167	1264	987	1549
1986	2471	1438	854	1643
1987	2719	1549	941	1856
1988	2586	1653	794	1658
1989	2346	1532	12593	

1 Draw block graphs to show these figures as clearly as possible.

2 The table only uses the number of units but does not show the cost. Why is this a better indicator of the amount of electricity used by the Johnsons' than showing the cost?

Mrs. Johnson also compiled a list of all the electrical appliances in the flat. She recorded the power rating of each one and generously estimated the number of hours each would be used during a week. She then multiplied the number of hours by 13 to get an estimate for a quarter.

```
 o                                              o
              ELECTRIC IRON

          MODEL NUMBER 6532/78

 240/220/110 V  AC      50/60 Hz      500 W

                 WARNING
      Before taking apart disconnect
      from mains by removing wall plug.
 o                                              o
```

Appliance	Power rating (watts)	Estimate (hours)	kW h (units)
Immersion heater	3 kW	100	300
Cooker	3 kW	70	
Washing machine	2 kW	60	
Household lighting	60 W	2000	
Iron	500 W	100	
Kettle	1 kW	100	
Hairdrier	500 W	20	
Refrigerator	100 W	500	
Mixer	500 W	10	
Television	100 W	400	
Radio	20 W	200	
Stereo	20 W	50	

The washing machine and immersion heater operate on the cheaper night rate tariff of 3 pence per unit, whilst the rest is charged at the normal rate of 6 pence per unit.

3 Complete the table by working out the estimated number of units for each appliance.

4 Using the two different tariffs for the appliances calculate the estimated cost.

5 Prepare a letter to be sent to the Electricity Board detailing your estimates, including tables and graphs to argue that it is unlikely that your family could possibly run up such a large bill. Point out the time of the year and suggest what might have happened to cause such a mistake.

Dear Sir,
    I would like to point out that the recent bill I received must be a mistake. From previous bills.........

Attainment
Target 11
**ELECTRICITY
AND
MAGNETISM**
Level 8

EXERCISE 41

Conductors

A thermistor can be used as a fire alarm. As it gets hotter its resistance decreases and more current can pass.

The circuit here shows how it can be used.

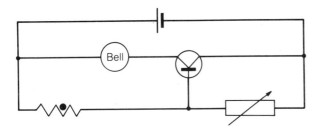

⇨**1** Label the components on the circuit diagram.

2 Find out how the bell can be switched on when the thermistor detects an increase in temperature.

3 Use the following information along with that above about the thermistor, to determine which of the four graphs represents the characteristics of which component.
● filament lamp – converts electrical energy into light and heat. As the temperature of the filament increases so does its resistance.
● ohmic conductor – has a fixed resistance, and does not vary with the current passing.
● diode valve – shows a variation in resistance according to the current flowing.

(a)
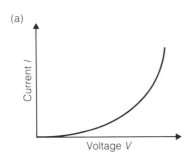

(b)
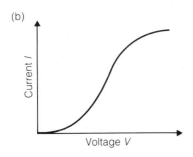

(c)
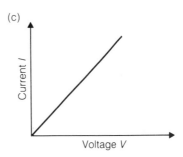

(d)
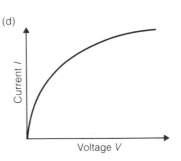

4 A filament lamp was investigated to see how its resistance varied with temperature. The results were as follows:

Temperature (°C)	Voltage V (volts)	Current I (amps)
50	1	
100	2	0.53
150	3	
200	4	0.89
250	5	
300	6	1.17
350	7	
400	8	1.39
450	9	
500	10	1.59

(a) Plot a current/voltage graph from the results in the table.
(b) Calculate the resistance of the filament for each temperature and plot a graph of temperature against resistance. Describe the pattern you see in your results.

Attainment
Target 11
**ELECTRICITY
AND
MAGNETISM**
Level 8

EXERCICE 42

Investigating a Circuit

The diagram shows one type of flashing indicator control unit that is found in some cars.

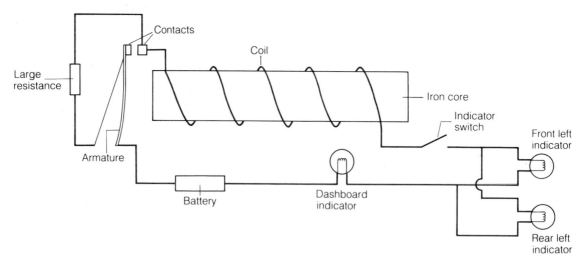

▷ **1** Examine the circuit diagram.

2 Cut out the boxes below . They are part of a flow chart which describes how the control unit works.

3 Arrange them in the correct order on a page. When you are sure of the order, stick them down. The arrows show the number of connections to each box, and the first box in the flow chart is shown in bold.

4 Normally the lamps flash between 60 and 120 times a minute. If one of the bulbs fuses, what happens to the current flowing through the resistance? How will this affect the flashing rate?

5 Change the circuit so that if an indicator bulb fuses, the dashboard light stays on all the time. Draw the part of the circuit you have changed.

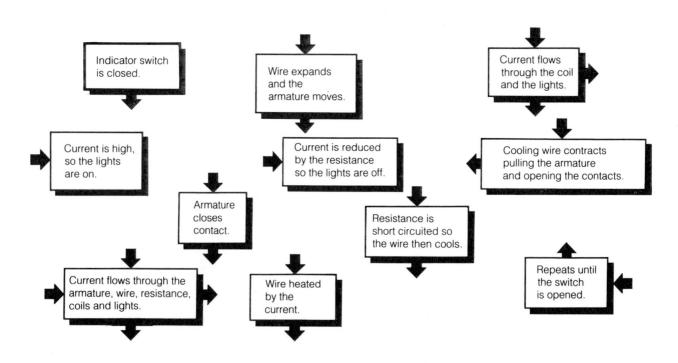

Attainment
Target 12
**INFORMATION
TECHNOLOGY**

Level 6

EXERCISE 43

Codes

Post offices have been helping us to communicate with each other since the last century. Now, sophisticated machines based on computer technology are used. More and more letters are being posted each year and delivering them becomes ever more challenging.

The letters are stacked and franked by machine.	Letters are automatically sorted into bundles for different destinations.	The machine 'reads' the bottom line of dots.
The letter is written, sealed and stamped.	Letters are passed to postal workers who read the postcode and 'write' the code electronically onto the letter. This consists of two rows of dots. The bottom row gives details of the sorting office to which it is being sent and the top row pinpoints the district where it is going.	Letters are fed into a machine, making sure they are the right way round and the right way up.
The letter is posted in the local post box.	The letter is collected and taken by van to the main sorting office.	First class letters are sorted from second class ones.
Letters for each particular destination are bagged and sent on their journey.	The letter is delivered to the address to which it was sent and read.	At the distant sorting office the letters are machine 'read' and sorted into bundles before being taken out.

➪ **1** The series of boxes above represent the stages involved from the point of writing and sending a letter to somebody receiving and reading it.
   (a) Make up a flow diagram to show the stages in the correct order.
   (b) Pretend you are the letter and describe what happens to you on your journey.

2 At which stage in this journey does a letter without a postcode have to be sorted by hand? Will this cause problems? If so, what might they be?

3 How many in your group know their postcode? Postcodes contain numbers and letters arranged in this way:

Letter(s)   Number(s)   Number   Letters

Example post code —— **SN15 2JT**

You can look up postcodes in local directories. Compare yours, if you know it, with the postcodes of the others in your group.

4 What are the advantages of using postcodes?

Attainment
Target 12
**INFORMATION
TECHNOLOGY**

Level 6

EXERCISE 44

Bar Codes

Packaged foods carry a unique bar code which identifies the manufacturer and the product. The bar code is made up of light and dark bars of various thicknesses. In some supermarkets the bar code can be read using a laser connected to a computer.

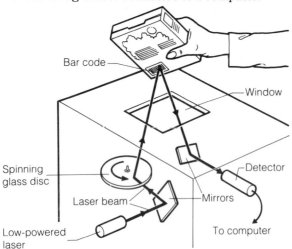

The laser beam passes through a revolving glass disc which deflects the beam along different paths as shown in the diagram. One beam should hit the bar code. The dark lines in the bar code absorb light, while the light lines reflect the light back through the window. The beam is reflected onto a detector which converts the light pattern to electrical impulses which are then sent to a computer.

1 Why is the spinning glass disc used?

2 The computer decodes the electrical signal to find out the manufacturer of the food, the type of food and the size of the package. The price is not found in the bar code. Where does the computer find this piece of information?

3 What other uses can the computer find for the information that it receives?

The bar codes below are from three manufacturers, Heinz, Batchelors and Napolina. The bar codes usually have the decoded numbers underneath them, so people can read them easily if necessary. The code is divided into two halves by three sets of longer lines.

Country of origin — Manufacturer code — Product code — Check digit

4 The laser checkout is very expensive. What advantages does it have for supermarkets? What are the advantages and disadvantages to the customer?

5 What is the manufacturer code for Heinz?

6 What is the code for Napolina?

7 Which country do you think has the code 50?

8 What is the purpose of having a check digit?

5 000157 004024
Heinz baked beans
Small tin

5 000157 004185
Heinz no added sugar
baked beans
Medium tin

5 000113 003979
Batchelors Slim-a-Soup
vegetable and beef

5 000157 004321
Heinz curried beans
Small tin

5 000232 190703
Princes kipper fillets
in brine

5 000232 430014
Princes fruit cocktail
Medium tin

5 000232 467010
Princes peeled
plum tomatoes
Big tin

5 000232 137302
Princes pineapple
pieces in juice

5 010061 001019
Napolina peeled
plum tomatoes
Medium tin

EXERCISE 45

Logic Gates (1)

Small electronic components are used as switches, called logic gates, inside a computer. There are only three basic types of logic gate called AND, OR and NOT gates. The workings of a logic gate can best be understood by drawing a truth table for that gate. A truth table shows whether a current is flowing in the wires connected to the logic gate. A Ø in the truth table means there is no electrical pulse at that point, while a 1 means there is an electrical pulse in that wire. The truth tables for the three logic gates are:

This is how they work:

AND gate – produces an output if both input wires carry an electrical impulse.

OR gate – produces an output if either of the input wires carries an electrical impulse.

NOT gate – produces an electrical impulse if the input wire does not carry an impulse, but does produce an output if the input wire does.

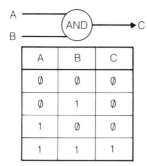

A	B	C
Ø	Ø	Ø
Ø	1	Ø
1	Ø	Ø
1	1	1

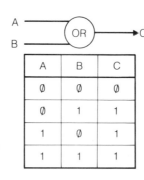

A	B	C
Ø	Ø	Ø
Ø	1	1
1	Ø	1
1	1	1

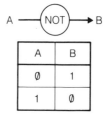

A	B
Ø	1
1	Ø

▷ Use the information in the three truth tables to complete the truth tables for the following circuits.

1

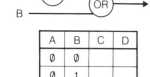

A	B	C	D
Ø	Ø		
Ø	1		
1	Ø		
1	1		

3

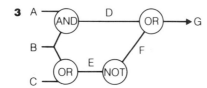

A	B	C	D	E	F	G
Ø	Ø	Ø				
Ø	Ø	1				
Ø	1	Ø				
Ø	1	1				
1	Ø	Ø				
1	Ø	1				
1		Ø				
1	1	1				

4

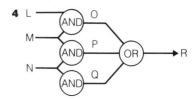

L	M	N	O	P	Q	R

2

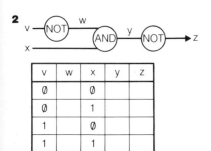

V	W	X	Y	Z
Ø		Ø		
Ø		1		
1		Ø		
1		1		

Attainment
Target 12
**INFORMATION
TECHNOLOGY**

Level 7

EXERCISE 46

Logic Gates (2)

There are other logic gates in common use apart from the AND, OR and NOT gates. These are called NAND and NOR.

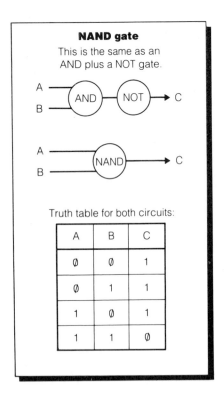

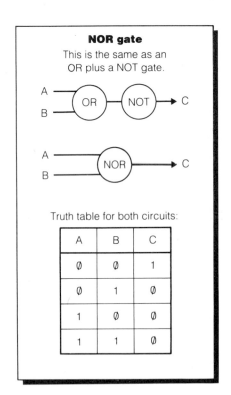

Computer manufacturers design circuits using large numbers of logic gates. In order to save both time and money they usually use only one type of gate connected in various ways. It is possible to combine NAND gates in such a way that they produce the equivalent of AND, OR, NOT or NOR gates. Similarly it is possible to combine NOR gates to produce the equivalent of AND, OR, NOT or NAND gates. The following three circuits are all the same and are the equivalent of an OR gate.

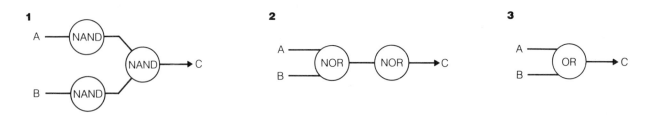

➪ **1** Construct truth tables for each circuit to show that they do produce the same output if they are given the same input.

2 Using NAND gates only, draw circuits which are equivalent to NOT, AND and NOR gates.

3 Using NOR gates only, draw circuits which are equivalent to NOT, AND and NAND gates.

ESSENTIAL SCIENCE ACTIVITIES © K. Bishop, W. Scott, D. Maddocks, 1990

Energy Sources

This diagram shows many of the sources of energy available to us and some of its uses.
There are gaps left in the diagram.

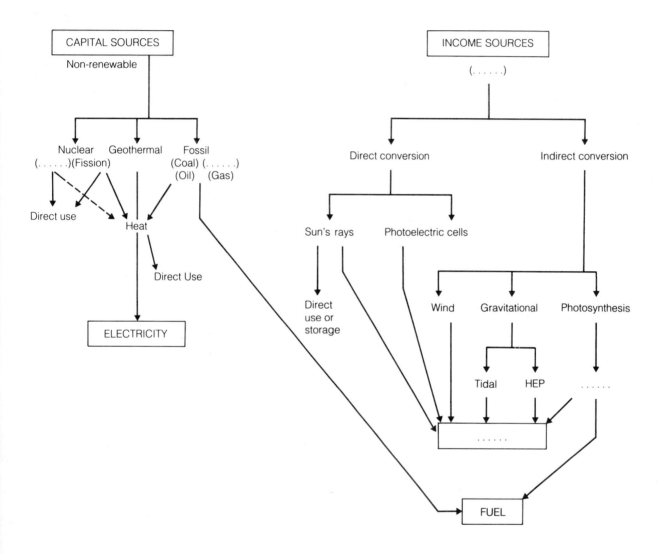

1 Use the following words to complete the diagram: fusion, peat, biomass, electricity, renewable.

2 Write down as many examples as you can of direct uses of the sun's rays.

3 Is it correct to say that hydroelectricity is produced from gravitational energy? Is there a part played by solar energy? If so, what is it?

4 List all the fuels mentioned on the diagram.

5 What is the meaning of the dotted arrow used on the diagram?

6 Why do you think the energy sources are called 'capital' and 'income'?

7 Indicate on the diagram where you would put magnetohydrodynamic generators and heat pumps.

ESSENTIAL SCIENCE ACTIVITIES © K. Bishop, W. Scott, D. Maddocks, 1990

Storage Heaters

Hot water tank

Night storage heaters and hot water tanks are two common ways in which energy is stored in the home. Both are designed to use cheap off-peak electricity during the night and make heat available for use during the day when electricity is much more expensive.

In night storage heaters, the cheap electricity is used to heat special bricks which cool slowly to release the heat during the day. These heaters are now very sophisticated. The amount of electrical energy taken in can be controlled and so can the rate at which heat is released. The new ones can automatically sense changes in temperature and take in more or less energy as required. In cold weather they will radiate heat from the face of the heater; in mild weather heat is released from vents in the top of the heater.

Storage heater

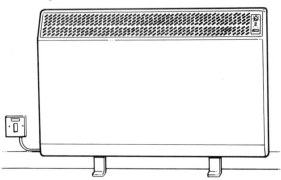

1 Why is night-time electricity called 'off-peak'? When do you think the peaks are?

2 Why is night-time electricity cheaper than day-time electricity? Does this difference in cost mean that it costs more to produce during the day?

3 What do you understand by the following words from the text:
(a) sophisticated
(b) automatically

4 Here are some typical data for an electric immersion heater hot water system:

> Hint:
>
> Energy used to heat the water (J) =
>
> mass of water x temperature change x 4200

Volume of the tank	150 litre (150 kg)
Cold water temperature	15 °C
Hot water temperature	65 °C
Amount of energy needed to raise the temperature of water by 1 °C	4200 joules
Number of joules in one unit of electricity (a kilowatt hour)	3 600 000 joules (3.6 MJ)

(a) Calculate how much electricity you use in heating all the water in the tank from 15 °C to 65 °C.
(b) Calculate how much this costs if electricity costs 6 pence per unit.

5 What else is heated up besides the water and what temperature does it reach?

6 In practice more electricity has to be used to keep the water at 65 °C because of the heat losses. With good insulation these losses can be kept to 10%. Re-calculate the electricity required taking into account that the losses are about 10%.

7 Some hot water tanks are fitted with two immersion heaters; a long one for use at night and a short one for day-time top up. Draw a diagram of such a tank showing where you would put the two heaters, and explain the reasons for putting them in those places. Also draw the water inlet and outlet pipes on the diagram.

EXERCISE 49

New Wave Power

The frightening prospect of global warming is making governments and scientists consider alternative energy sources which do not release vast quantities of carbon dioxide into the atmosphere or produce waste which cannot be disposed of.

Researchers at Queen's University, Belfast have built a prototype of a wave power generator on the rocky shore of Islay, an island off the Atlantic coast of Scotland.

The machine is designed to make use of both the ebb and the flow of the rollers coming in off the Atlantic. It uses them to compress air which then drives a turbine. When it is connected to a generator it can produce 40 kW of electricity. This is enough for a small village. Given time the researchers expect to be able to build a wave power generator capable of producing 1500 kW. At the moment the Isle of Islay relies on expensive imports of diesel fuel.

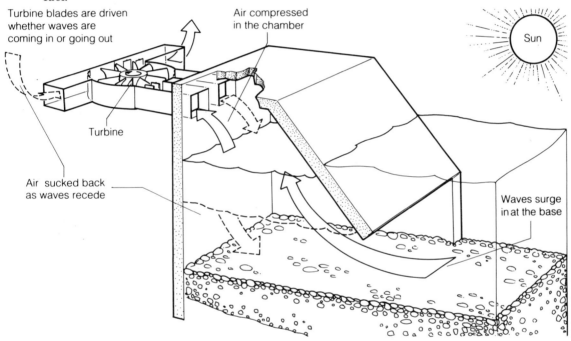

Turbine blades are driven whether waves are coming in or going out

Air compressed in the chamber

Sun

Turbine

Air sucked back as waves recede

Waves surge in at the base

Wind turbine generators on Burgar Hill, Orkney

▷ **1** Wave power is said to be an example of solar power. Explain why this is.

2 Wind generators are also examples of solar power. Explain the advantages and disadvantages of this kind of power generation.

3 The wave power generator is used to compress air. Draw a flow diagram to show the stages involved starting with the sun and finishing with the distribution of electricity to homes on the island. Show all the energy changes.

4 It will not be possible to use wave or wind power generators to replace major power stations. Explain why not and suggest what kind of situations or locations would be ideal for a) wave power, and b) wind power.

5 Why is this type of power generation described as renewable?

Energy Conservation

The conservation of energy is the best way to reduce energy consumption. Uninsulated houses lose vast amounts of heat. Knowing this, many double glazing, loft insulation and cavity-wall insulation companies advertise extensively through the media.

Double glazing is probably the most expensive of the different forms of house insulation. Companies advertise that great savings can be made through the installation of double glazing, but is it really cost-effective?

Generally speaking, heat loss directly through window surfaces is about 10 per cent. Double glazing companies claim that heat losses can be cut by half. If this is so then half that 10 per cent loss can be saved, that is 5 per cent. The cost of a 250 cm × 120 cm double glazed window could be anywhere from £300 to £600. Double glazing for a whole house could cost from £1500 to £3000.

A consumer survey in 1988 produced a list of energy saving best-buys.
1 Roof insulation
2 Draught exclusion
3 Cavity wall insulation
4 Double glazing
5 Solid wall insulation and under floor insulation

An average cost for heating an uninsulated house is around £600 per year. To find out how cost effective a form of insulation is you need to be able to calculate how many years it will take for the insulation to pay for itself in savings on the heating bills – known as pay-back time.

$$\text{pay-back time} = \frac{\text{total cost of installation}}{\text{savings per year}}$$

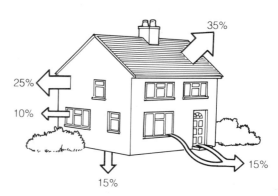

Typical heat losses from a post-war house

➡ **1** Work out what the pay-back times would be for each of the following installations assuming that heating for a year costs £600 and that each type of installation reduces heat losses by half that shown on the diagram.

Installation	Total cost (£)
roof insulation	250
draught exclusion	100
cavity wall	750
double glazing	2000

2 What kind of insulation does your home have? Can you make a recommendation for the most cost-effective way of improving the insulation?

3 If you were involved in some community work and came across old people living in a poorly insulated house, advise on the most effective forms of insulation that they might be able to afford on a low income.

4 Hypothermia is a problem encountered by many old people. Find out what it is, and how it can best be prevented.

Measuring Food Energy

All kinds of journals dealing with diet, fitness and health, as well as newspapers and magazines offer calorie charts which tell you the energy value of a whole range of different foods. But have you ever thought where the figures came from?

To find out the energy value of a food you have to burn it completely and measure the amount of heat energy it releases. The instrument used to do this is called a bomb calorimeter.

The principle of the bomb calorimeter is that it allows total combustion of the food so that all of the food's energy is transferred to the water surrounding the bomb. If the amount of electrical energy put in to start the process of combustion is known then the energy value of the food can be calculated from the rise in temperature of the surrounding water.

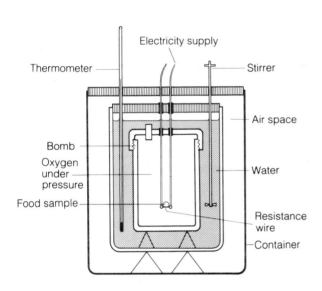

A bomb calorimeter

▷ **1** The passage in the box describes what a bomb calorimeter is and how it works. However there are gaps in this passage shown by asterisks (*). Copy it out and use the diagram of the apparatus to help you fill in the gaps.

Now answer the following questions about the design of the bomb and how the energy value of the food is calculated.

2 Why do you think the bomb contains pure oxygen under pressure?

3 What are the advantages of providing the initial energy in the form of electricity?

4 If you were designing the bomb itself, what features would you make sure it had?

5 What are the two readings required from the thermometer?

6 What other pieces of information are needed about the water?

The bomb is made of a metal case with a screw lid. A known amount of   *   is placed inside the bomb which is then filled with   *   . The bomb is put inside a   *   container filled with   *   which contains a   *   and a stirrer. The bomb is insulated from the bottom of the container and is surrounded by an   *   space. The food is   *   by an electric current. The heat released by the food warms up the surrounding   *   . If the amount of   *   energy used in the first place is known, and this is subtracted from the amount of   *   produced, it is possible to calculate the   *   value of the   *   .

ESSENTIAL SCIENCE ACTIVITIES   © K. Bishop, W. Scott, D. Maddocks, 1990

In the Gym

Erica was intent on carrying out a thoroughly scientifically-based weight-training programme. Her aim was to exercise her body and keep a record of all she did each day.

For each exercise she calculated the work done and the power she generated in that time. By drawing graphs she reckoned she could then visualise her progress more clearly.

This was her record of achievement for a week:

Day	Left arm lift				Right arm lift				Left leg lift				Right leg lift			
	mass (kg)	distance (m)	lifts	time (s)	mass (kg)	distance (m)	lifts	time (s)	mass (kg)	distance (m)	lifts	time (s)	mass (kg)	distance (m)	lifts	time (s)
Monday	12	0.8	25	30	12	0.8	25	32	12	0.6	25	35	12	0.6	25	37
Tuesday	12	0.8	25	26	12	0.8	25	29	12	0.6	25	32	12	0.6	25	33
Wednesday	12	0.8	25	23	12	0.8	25	27	12	0.6	25	30	12	0.6	25	31
Thursday	12	0.8	25	21	12	0.8	25	25	12	0.6	25	28	12	0.6	25	29
Friday	12	0.8	25	20	12	0.8	25	24	12	0.6	25	27	12	0.6	25	29
Saturday	12	0.8	25	20	12	0.8	25	23	12	0.6	25	27	12	0.6	25	28
Sunday	12	0.8	25	19	12	0.8	25	22	12	0.6	25	26	12	0.6	25	28

1 Use the pattern:

work done (J) = force (N) x vertical distance (m)

to calculate the work done by each of Eric's four limbs. (1kg is roughly 10 Newtons.)

2 Now use the pattern:

$$power (W) = \frac{work\ done\ (J)}{time\ (s)}$$

to calculate the power developed by each limb for each day.

3 Plot a graph, for each of the limbs, of power developed against day of the week.

Power/W

Day of the week

Power developed in left arm

4 Compare the progress made by the limbs and comment on any patterns you see in the results.

5 Suggest how Erica might further develop her programme of training.

6 Explain why Erica's calculations depend on doing vertical lifts.

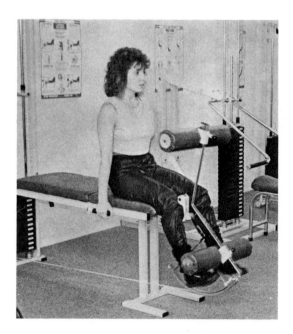

Comparing Sounds

The ear is an organ that detects sounds, converts them to electrical impulses and passes them on to the brain where they are interpreted and made sense of. In some ways it is like a public address (PA) system. The passage that follows describes how a PA system works.

> The microphone is an instrument that detects the movement of sound waves. A tiny moving coil in the head of the microphone detects this movement and depending on the kind of sound waves sends a tiny changing electric current along the microphone to the amplifier. This current represents the pitch and volume of the sound. The amplifier magnifies the tiny changing electric currents so that a much bigger signal can be sent to the speakers. The speakers then reverse the process carried out by the microphone and convert the changing electric currents into sound waves. This is the sound we hear from the speakers.

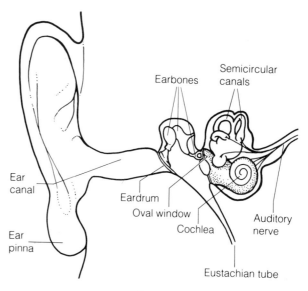

The ear

1 Complete the table by filling in answers 1–8 and putting ticks in the right hand column. You will need to look at the diagrams of the structure of the ear and the PA system.

Ear	PA system	Tick where you think the comparison is good, fair or poor		
		good	fair	poor
ear pinna	1...............			
ear canal	2...............			
3...............	moving coil in microphone			
4...............	microphone head			
ear bones	5...............			
cochlea	6...............			
auditory nerve	7...............			
8...............	speaker leads			

2 In each case where you think the comparison is poor explain your reasoning.

3 Write a short account which criticises the comparison of the ear with a PA system. Make sure you consider the following points in your answer:

(a) do the two systems have the same function?
(b) how similar are the systems in the way they detect and amplify pitch?
(c) what is the role of the brain in the functioning of the ear?

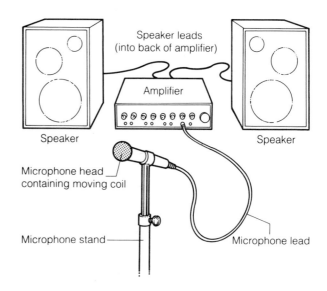

A public address (PA) system

Attainment
Target 14
**SOUND AND
MUSIC**

Level 8–9

EXERCISE 54

Samplers

Musical instruments produce notes which vary in pitch, loudness and tone quality. Samplers are electronic machines which can 'sample' the sounds that a musical instrument makes and convert them into digital form. The sound can then be reproduced through the keyboard. The saxophone is typical of the sort of instrument which can be successfully sampled.

When a vibrating tuning fork is held in front of a microphone a pure waveform is seen on an oscilloscope. This diagram shows the waveform that a concert A (440 Hz) tuning fork would produce.

Tuning fork

▷ **1** Look at this waveform produced by a tuning fork. What is changing in this wave and what remains the same? Describe what you would hear.

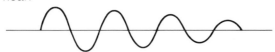

Even when they play the same note, wind and string instruments produce quite different waveforms. This is because their tone qualities are very different. Tone quality depends on the harmonics which are present as well as the basic waveform. This diagram is typical of a violin waveform.

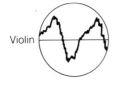

Violin

2 What do you think gives musical instruments their characteristic tone qualities?

A sampler analyses a waveform of a musical instrument and converts it into digital form. This is how it would sample a tuning fork note sampling eight times per wavelength.

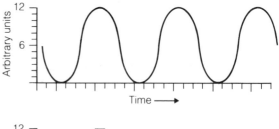

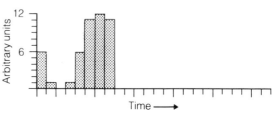

3 Copy and complete the digital form of the waveform.

4 Draw the digital form using the trace below obtained from a stringed instrument.

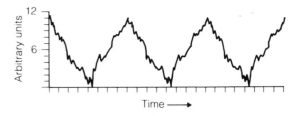

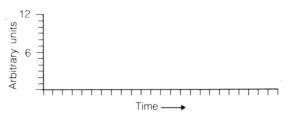

5 Explain why, in this case, it is necessary to increase the number of samples taken per wavelength.

Attainment
Target 15
**USING LIGHT
AND ELECTRO-
MAGNETIC
RADIATION**
Level 7

EXERCISE 55

Fibre Optics

Fibre optics have revolutionised telephone and television communications. This newspaper article describes how they work.

What are fibre optics?

Scientists have been aware for a long time of the possibility of communicating by light. The invention of the laser as a new light source stimulated fresh ideas and led to the proposal in the mid 1960s of transmitting signals through very thin glass fibres. The glass fibre needs to be of the purest quality otherwise the light beams passing through it would be adversely affected by the alien particles. In fact, so clean must the glass fibre be that its impurities over a kilometre must be no more than those present in a few millimetres of ordinary glass.

Within a few years of that first proposal, fibre of sufficient quality had been made, and transmission of telecommunications signals by light had become a practical possibility. To make such fibre, pure silica or glass has to be heated to well over 1000 °C at which it becomes molten, or even vaporises. Special compounds are added to change the refractive index and then a rod is made which has an inner core and an outer cladding layer.

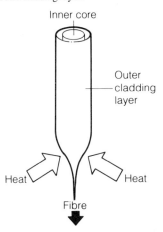

Production of an optical fibre

The rod is heated at its base and pulled out into an ultra-fine fibre of the same construction. Finally, to protect it from being scratched, the fibre is coated with a fine layer of polymer plastic.

An optical fibre therefore consists of two very thin glass rods, one inside the other, the inner core having a slightly higher refractive index than the outer layer. Light beamed into this central core will be trapped by the outer layer, and will bounce off it (on the principle of total internal reflection), zig-zagging all the way down the fibre.

Even if the fibre is bent into a loop, light will still bounce along the inner core, though some may be lost into the outer core.

Hand in hand with the further development of optical fibres and light sources comes the need for engineers to design two new types of equipment: optical transmitters to take in the electrical signals carrying telephone calls or television pictures, and to convert them into equivalent light signals to feed down the fibre; and optical receivers to convert the incoming light signals back to their conventional electrical forms, which are then able to operate the telephone or television or go back into the telephone communications network.

Why are engineers so keen to use optical fibres? Already some of the telephone traffic between Britain's cities is being carried by optical fibres and at the other extreme, fibres are used to carry information in short links between computers. Probably their major advantage is their ability to carry a signal without amplification, for longer distances than conventional cables, which need to be electronically boosted by 'repeaters' every two kilometres. The record in Britain so far is 102 km. Light carries information much farther in fibre than electricity does in a conventional cable. Another benefit is that fibre optic cable is smaller and lighter. A pair of fibres can already carry 2000 telephone calls simultaneously. This means that the existing crowded ducts running beneath our streets can be more economically used – a 10-fibre cable is about the size of a single co-axial cable. Also, the present telephone system is based on the use of copper cables – and copper is becoming increasingly expensive. In fact, the largest single expense in any telephone system is the cable, which is why telephone engineers are constantly looking for cheaper ways to send messages.

Optical fibres are also free from interference such as that caused by electrical machinery, radio broadcasting and the high voltage surge that can be induced by lightning and cause so much damage. An optical fibre cable buried in the road will not be affected by ordinary cables lying beside it, unlike conventional cables.

All sorts of experiments are being undertaken to examine the applications of fibre optics in hospital machinery and surgical equipment, underwater communications, security fencing and electrical generation.

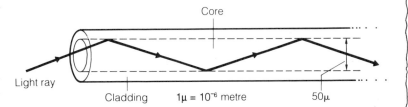

Optical fibre showing total internal reflection

Core

Light ray

Cladding $1\mu = 10^{-6}$ metre 50μ

➪ **1** Rewrite this newspaper article in less than two hundred words. You will first need to decide which points are essential and then make a list. You must explain what fibre optics are and why they represent a great advance in communications technology.

2 What characteristic is essential in the manufacture of optical fibres?

3 Explain the meaning of 'total internal reflection'. Give another example of this phenomenon.

4 Find out why optical fibres are not interfered with by electrical appliances.

5 Carry out your own research to find other applications of fibre optic technology.

Attainment
Target 15
**USING LIGHT
AND ELECTRO-
MAGNETIC
RADIATION**
Level 7

EXERCISE 56

Colour TV

Colour television did not become widely available to viewers in the UK until the 1970s. But, as early as 1928 John Logie Baird, the Scottish inventor, had demonstrated colour TV in action. The following passage is a description of the system he used.

Baird used a Nipkow disk to scan his picture image. This disc had a set of holes arranged in a spiral round its outer edges. Each hole had red, green and blue filters in it. The disc was spun quickly and, in turn, each hole scanned across the picture. Each hole scanned across a piece of the picture slightly lower than the previous hole. In this way, the whole picture was scanned.

The light passing through each filter was focussed onto one of three photoelectric cells. As the light intensity falling on each cell varied, so did the current produced by the cell. These three signals were sent to a receiver. At the receiver the signals were fed to three discharge tubes containing helium, mercury and neon. The varying current produced varying light intensities in the discharge tubes. The light from these tubes was focussed through holes in another Nipkow disc onto a screen. The disc had to be rotating in exactly the same way as the one in the camera which scanned the picture. In this way, the two discs were synchronised and the original picture was built up in lines by the scanning of the spiral of holes across the screen.

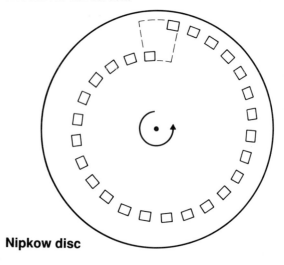

Nipkow disc

⇨ **1** Read the passage and note down as many similarities and differences as you can between the Baird system and our modern one.

2 Which of the three discharge tubes gave the red light in the picture?

3 Our TVs have 625 lines in their picture. How many has Baird's? What does this tell you about the quality of the picture Baird produced?

4 If the drawing of the disc above is 5 times too small, what was the biggest size of picture that could be transmitted?

5 Explain why it was not possible to transmit larger pictures with this disc.

6 What are the main disadvantages of Baird's system?

Attainment
Target 15
**USING LIGHT
AND ELECTRO-
MAGNETIC
RADIATION**
Level 7

EXERCISE 57

Cat's-eyes

Cat's-eyes are found at the centre and edges of roads. They reflect light from headlamps to give drivers a better idea of the position of the road.

The cat's-eye itself is a glass cylinder in a convex lens and the rear is a mirror. The lens and the mirror share the same focal point.

The diagrams show two parallel beams of light striking a cat's-eye.

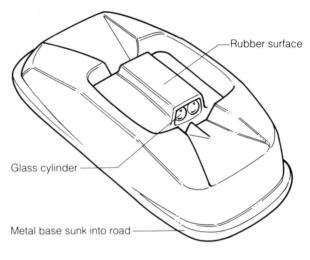

Rubber surface

Glass cylinder

Metal base sunk into road

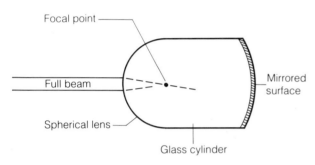

Focal point

Full beam

Spherical lens

Mirrored surface

Glass cylinder

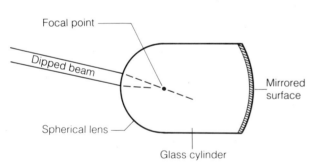

Focal point

Dipped beam

Spherical lens

Mirrored surface

Glass cylinder

▷ **1** Complete the dotted lines to show the light path into the cat's-eye to the mirrored rear surface. Show the return path of light using a different coloured pencil.

2 Where does the returning beam of light go? Why does this make the cat's-eye useful?

3 Some cat's-eyes are tinted green, yellow or red. Find out where you might see each colour and what they mean.

4 Cat's-eyes are now being replaced in certain parts of Great Britain. What is being used in their place?

Attainment
Target 15
**USING LIGHT
AND ELECTRO-
MAGNETIC
RADIATION**
Level 7

EXERCISE 58

Roasting in the Sun

Solar spectrum
Visible

UVA UVB

IR

Sun

Short ⟶ Longer wavelength

UVA

UVB

Visible

IR

- Roasting in the sun like a chicken on a spit is many people's idea of heaven. Britain's uncertain climate makes people flock to places like the Mediterranean where they suddenly expose their lily-white skin to the ferocity of the sun's potent radiation.

- 1000 people in the UK die each year from a form of skin cancer known as malignant melanoma.

- Skin naturally produces a dark pigment called melanin which absorbs harmful UV radiation. UV light consists of UVA and UVB light.

- Sun protection factors and sun blocks are chemical screens, (dibenzoyl methane), which absorb UVB and prevent burning.

- Skin needs sunlight to synthesise vitamin D, essential for good bone formation.

- UVA is better blocked by titanium dioxide which reflects it.

- Fair skinned people moving to the tropics are more susceptible to skin cancer than native dark skinned people.

- Dark skinned people already have melanin in the skin to absorb UV radiation.

- Skin needs to acclimatise to sunlight. It takes time to produce melanin. Cover up or sit in the shade and expose the skin gradually over a period of time.

- Most at risk are the sunseekers who normally work indoors.

- UV radiation can produce cataracts in the eyes.

⇨ **1** Use the information to draw a poster which describes the dangers of overexposure to the sun's radiation.

2 Write an article for a youth magazine which indicates the dangers that white skinned people can be exposed to by excessive sunbathing.

Attainment
Target 16
**THE EARTH IN
SPACE**

Level 6

EXERCISE 59

Speed of Light

Light travels through space at a constant speed of 300 000 kilometres per second (3×10^5 km/s). The time taken for light to travel from one object to another, therefore, depends on how far apart the objects are. *Use the data here to help you solve the puzzles set out below.*

Object	Mean distance from the Sun (million km)
Earth	150
Mars	228
Jupiter	1778
Pluto	5900

1 How many minutes does it take a burst of sunlight to reach an observer on the Earth?

2 When the Sun, Earth and Jupiter are directly in line how long would it take for a pulse of laser light to travel from the Earth to Jupiter? There are two answers to this question, both of which are correct. Try to work out both of them.

3 This question does not have enough information for you to answer it:

How long would it take for a radio signal from a satellite orbiting Mars to travel back to a receiver on Earth?

(a) Draw a diagram to explain why you cannot answer this question.
(b) What extra information do you need in order to answer it?

4 Two people have seen your answer to question 1. One says it is too large and the other says it is too small. Explain how all three of you might be correct. You will find it useful to draw a diagram.

Distances between stars are so large that a special, very large unit is needed. This is called a light-year. One light-year is the distance travelled by light in one year (365 days).

5 The very bright star Sirius is 9 light-years away from us. How many kilometres is this?

6 Pluto is 5 900 000 000 km from the Earth. As this is a very large number calculate it in light-years.

7 When you look at a constellation, such as Orion, all the stars seem to be the same distance away. But they are not. Draw the shape you think the constellation would have if it was viewed from a planet orbiting Betelgeuse. What other information do you need to be certain that the shape of your drawing is correct?

The data here concern the masses and volumes of the planets in the Solar sytem. The units, however, are not the ones you might expect.

Planet	Mass	Volume
Mercury	0.056	0.06
Venus	0.815	0.88
Earth	1.0	1.0
Mars	0.11	0.15
Jupiter	317.9	1320.0
Saturn	95.1	755.0
Uranus	14.5	67.1
Neptune	17.2	57.0

8 Calculate the density of each of the planets by using the following pattern:

$$\text{density} = \frac{\text{mass}}{\text{volume}}$$

9 What name could you devise to give to this unit of density?

10 Arrange the planets in two groups according to their densities. You will find that one of the planets does not fit exactly into either group. Nevertheless, choose one of the groups to put it into and give a reason for choosing it.

11 What is it about the composition of a planet that decides which group it falls into?

12 From what you know of Pluto, which group would you expect it to be in? Give a reason for your answer.

EXERCISE 60

Other Planets

The following passage is part of a description of the planet Venus. It was written for a magazine. The author has asked you to read it and check the spelling, punctuation and information and to check that it makes sense.

THE PLANET VENUS

In some ways Venus is very simalar to the Earth. It's size volume and weight are about the same as the Earth, as is its density.

In other ways Venus and the Earth are quiet different. For example, we couldnt live there. Its atmosphere contains Carbon Monoxide and sulphuric acid Vapour and it is very hot. It is hot for too reasons: Firstly, it's more nearer the sun than we are – only 67 million kilometres and, secondly, its dense clouds keep the suns heat trapped near the planet's surface.

Both Americans and the Soviets have sent probes to Benus. The USA Pioneer mission went in 1978 and Soviet Venera space craft orbited the planet in The two used radar to map the surface of the planet 1984. and sent back much mored etailed pictures than before about the planet. The Soviets released baloons into the venusian atmosphere as there spacecraft flew past the planet to meet halley's comet in1985. The Americans plan to send a very sensitive radar mapping satellite to the planet at the end of the decade.

When these space photography missions are compleat we shall no much more about our nearest neighbour.

▷ **1** Read the passage, number the lines and write a report on it. In your report refer to the lines where you feel there are errors or problems.

A spaceprobe landed on a distant planet in the Megagamma galaxy and several experiments were carried out on the atmosphere. This is a description of one of those experiments.

200 g of the atmosphere was analysed. Its mass when dry was only 180 g. 60 g of this was found to be oxygen and three-quarters of the rest was nitrogen. The remaining 30g of atmosphere contained three gases: two-thirds was the inert gas argon, 20% was carbon dioxide and the third gas was carbon monoxide.

2 Use this information to complete the summary below.

Summary

Mass of atmosphere = 200 g
Mass of dry atmosphere = 180 g
Mass of water =
Mass of oxygen = 60 g
Mass of nitrogen =
Mass of argon =
Mass of carbon dioxide =
Mass of carbon monoxide =

3 Work out the percentage of each component present and represent the information as a pie graph.

4 Write a few lines to describe the main differences between the composition of the atmosphere of the Earth and the atmosphere of the planet in the Megagamma galaxy.

5 List a few other pieces of information you would need to do a complete comparison of the atmospheres.

6 Is the atmosphere on the planet safe to breathe? Give reasons to support your answer.

7 What would the main differences be between a fire on Earth and a fire on this distant planet?

Attainment
Target 17
**THE NATURE
OF SCIENCE**

Level 8

EXERCISE 61

Cold Fusion

Energy for free! That is a cry few scientists believe any more. Nevertheless that was what was reported in the papers when Professors Fleischmann and Pons announced the results of their research into cold nuclear fusion at Utah University in the USA.

Fusion is the process that generates heat energy within the Sun. By definition fusion produces heat energy by combining small atoms to make larger ones and in the Sun produces temperatures of millions of degrees Celsius. For years scientists trying to imitate the process have themselves used very high temperatures. The Joint European Torus (JET), based near Oxford, represents one research project attempting to obtain useful energy from this process – so far unsuccessfully.

➪ **1** Explain why trying to generate energy by nuclear fusion is likely to be a very hard problem to solve.

2 Find out about the progress of these different research projects and assess the likelihood of nuclear fusion becoming a serious alternative to conventional sources of energy.

Professors Fleischmann and Pons are electro-chemists. Recently they reported that they generated heat energy in a 'test-tube' process which they claim was nuclear fusion.

The remarkable thing was that their experiment was done at room temperature. Normally the barriers between atomic nuclei will not allow them to come close enough to fuse. Only very high temperatures

can make this happen. In the Fleischmann-Pons experiment an electric current was passed between two palladium electrodes immersed in an electrolyte containing 'heavy' water (deuterium oxide). Just as in the electrolysis of water where hydrogen atoms move to the cathode, it is thought that 'heavy' hydrogen atoms pack into the palladium cathode and fuse to form helium atoms. Pons and Fleischmann reckon that the reaction generated 4 watts for every 1 watt consumed and produced tritium and neutrons, the expected products of nuclear fusion.

French scientist with apparatus to investigate the results of Fleischmann and Pons

3 Write a balanced equation for the laboratory electrolysis of water. Write a second one to show how heavy hydrogen could be liberated from heavy water.

4 Deuterium and tritium are isotopes of hydrogen which contain neutrons. Use diagrams to show the atomic structure of all three isotopes.

5 Write a balanced equation to show what happens when two atoms of deuterium fuse to form an atom of helium.

6 The theory of the cold fusion reaction is that the heavy hydrogen atoms pack, under pressure, into the palladium lattice and fuse. What scientific principle does this show?

7 There are virtually unlimited supplies of heavy water in the oceans but it has to be extracted. The process of extraction involves the liberation of large quantities of hydrogen. What could this be used for?

8 The results of the Fleischmann-Pons experiment show an energy output of four times the input. Why are other scientists still very sceptical about these results?

9 As yet no one has repeated the Fleischmann-Pons experiment. Why is it important for scientists throughout the world to try to repeat the results?

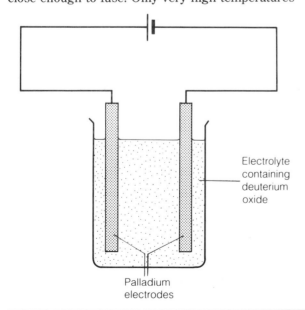

Electrolyte containing deuterium oxide

Palladium electrodes

Attainment
Target 2
**THE VARIETY
OF LIFE**

Level 8

PRACTICAL 1

Treating Used Water

The quality of our drinking water and the safety of our beaches for bathing are highly topical issues at the moment. The EC (European Community) wants all member countries to reach the same standard. Water treatment, however, is notoriously expensive. Used water from domestic houses contains washing-up liquid, cleaning water, bath water and sewage. Used water from industry can also contain heavy metals and other toxic substances. All this passes to a sewage works where the water is treated before being discharged back into rivers or the sea.

A sewage treatment works

Water treatment consists of passing the water through a series of tanks which filter the sewage and remove large particles. In most sewage works the sludge produced has oxygen bubbled through it. In this experiment you are going to investigate this method of treatment and see what effect the oxygen has.

Equipment

- two gas jars and lids
- aquarium aerator
- Vaseline
- air pipe
- farmyard or garden manure

Procedure

1 Place a small amount of farmyard manure or garden manure into each gas jar.
2 Fill each jar to three-quarters full with tap water.
3 Grease a lid with Vaseline and place it on one of the gas jars.
4 Connect an air pipe to an aerator and bubble air through the second gas jar.
5 Place both jars in a fume cupboard.
6 Leave for at least one week.
7 Examine the jars and their contents.

Results

Draw up a table which compares what has happened to the two gas jars. In particular, describe their appearance and smell.

Discussion

1 What difference did the aerating of the manure make?

2 The aeration provides oxygen for bacteria. Where do these bacteria come from and why do they need oxygen?

3 What do these bacteria do in the manure?

4 Explain why the sewage works uses an aeration process.

5 Raw sewage is sometimes released straight into the rivers or pumped through long pipes out to sea. What are the objections to this?

6 The waste from sewage works is called 'sludge'. It is possible to use it as a fertiliser but there are problems. What has to be removed from the sludge before it can be used as a fertiliser?

Dumping sewage sludge at sea

7 British sludge is also dumped out at sea. Environmental groups are opposed to this. Why do you think the British do this whereas other countries do not. What environmental damage could it do?

ESSENTIAL SCIENCE ACTIVITIES © K. Bishop, W. Scott, D. Maddocks, 1990

Attainment
Target 2
**THE VARIETY
OF LIFE**

Level 8

PRACTICAL 2

Effects of a Sewage Works

A sewage works must, by law, remove and treat sewage before discharging the treated water into a river. This treated water could then pass down the river and be used for another town's drinking supply. Animals and plants that live in the river help to clean up the water. The purpose of this investigation is to study the effects of pollution in a local water course.

Equipment

- Four 400 cm³ conical flasks and corks
- 250 cm³ beaker
- test tubes
- test tube rack
- filter funnel and papers
- oxygen meter
- Nessler's reagent

Procedure

1 Obtain four samples of water from the river that your local sewage works discharges into, and one sample from the tap which you can use as a control. Take your samples from:
- just above the works
- just below the works
- 500 m down river from the works
- 2 km down river
- tap water.

2 Perform the following tests on each sample.
(a) Smell – put a sample in a corked flask for 48 hours, then smell it carefully.

(b) Detergents – put 50 cm³ of the sample in a 400 cm³ conical flask. Shake the flask vigorously for one minute. Time how long the bubbles last on the surface to get an indication of the amount of detergent present in the water.

(c) Suspended solids – shake 50 cm³ of the sample in a test tube, then filter it. Open out the filter papers and compare them.

(d) Ammonia – put 50 cm³ of the sample in a beaker. Add 2 cm³ of Nessler's reagent. A yellow colour shows ammonia is present. The more ammonia there is, the darker is the colour.

(e) Oxygen – use an oxygen meter if available. If not, your teacher may demonstrate a chemical test.

Results

Present all your results in a table.

Discussion

1 Summarise the greatest differences between the water upstream from the sewage works and the water downstream.

2 Make a visual comparison between the water above and below the sewage works. Is there any link between what you see and the results from your tests on the water? Note the following points: water colour, foam, plants along the banks and plants in the river.

3 If the river is fairly slow moving and shallow you may be able to use a net to sample the animals present. If possible sample at the four collecting points. Explain how animals might be used to indicate the presence of pollution.

4 The following animals are indicator species. Find out whether they indicate high or low water quality.

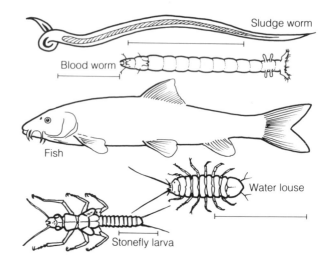

5 Use your results to make a display which shows the quality of the river water.

PRACTICAL 3
Investigating Microbes in Water

In the summer of 1989, a message from the Thames Water Authority was flashed up on people's television screens in the Oxford and Swindon area warning that all water must be boiled for at least two minutes before being given to babies. It turned out that a microscopic parasite, called *Cryptosporidia*, was responsible for a disease causing diarrhoea and vomiting. A government inquiry was then set up to investigate the source. This was suspected of being a farm waste such as slurry, although no leaks had been reported at the time.

Poor sanitation can also lead to the contamination of water supplies. Diseases such as cholera and typhoid, for instance, are known to be transmitted in water. It is possible to test water supplies for possible contamination with sewage by using a special broth or agar which changes colour when sewage bacteria are present.

Equipment

☐ MacConkey bottles of red broth

☐ sterile loop

☐ bottle of sterile water (control)

☐ collected samples of water to be tested

☐ nutrient agar plates

☐ chinagraph pencil

☐ incubator set at 37 °C

Procedure

You are provided with a series of numbered water samples which you are going to test for the presence of sewage bacteria. The bottle marked control contains sterile water.

Broth test – the broth turns yellow if sewage bacteria are present.
1 Label one bottle of MacConkey red broth as control.
2 Sterilise the inoculation loop in a Bunsen flame.
3 Dip the loop into the water sample marked 'control' and then into the bottle of broth. Repeat steps 2 and 3 twice more.
4 Replace the caps on the bottles.
5 Store the bottle of broth in an incubator set at 37 °C for 24 hours.
6 Repeat steps 1 to 5 for each water sample.

Agar test – pink colonies of bacteria indicate the presence of sewage bacteria.
1 Use a chinagraph pencil to divide the base of the agar plate into segments and add your name.

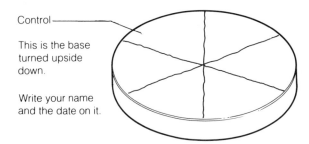

Control ——

This is the base turned upside down.

Write your name and the date on it.

2 Sterilise the inoculation loop in a Bunsen flame.
3 Dip the loop into the water sample marked 'control' and then streak it carefully, without cutting into the agar, in the corresponding segment.
4 Replace the cap on the bottle.
5 Repeat steps 2 to 4 for each water sample.
6 Incubate the plate in an incubator set at 37 °C for 24 hours.

Results

Use the headings below to complete a table of your results.

Water sample	Broth colour	Colour of agar bacterial colonies
control		

Discussion

1 Comment on the water quality of each sample. Your teacher will tell you where each sample came from.

2 Which other water supplies would it be of interest to you to test?

3 Water said to be fit for drinking is called potable. It is the job of the Water Companies to provide potable water for consumers. Why is it important that they should regularly test all water supplies?

4 If you were in a country where you were not sure of the quality of the drinking water what precautions might you take before drinking it?

Attainment
Target 3
**PROCESSES
OF LIFE**

Level 7

PRACTICAL 4

Digesting Food

Digestion is the breakdown of large food molecules into small ones which can be absorbed into the bloodstream. The breakdown is speeded up by enzymes which are released into the small intestine. An enzyme called amylase speeds up the breakdown of starch to glucose.

In this investigation you are going to design an experiment to simulate the process and conditions that occur in the human digestive system.

Before you start, your group must agree a theory about what will happen. Only then can you design the procedure. It is assumed that you know how to carry out tests for starch and glucose.

Equipment

- ☐ 10 cm length of narrow (1 cm) Visking tubing
- ☐ 25 cm³ measuring cylinder or 5 cm³ syringe
- ☐ three 150 cm³ beakers
- ☐ boiling tubes
- ☐ test tubes
- ☐ test tube rack
- ☐ cotton
- ☐ starch solution
- ☐ amylase (enzyme) solution
- ☐ stop clock
- ☐ Benedict's reagent
- ☐ iodine solution
- ☐ spotting tile
- ☐ thermometer

Procedure

1 Collect the equipment shown in the diagram.

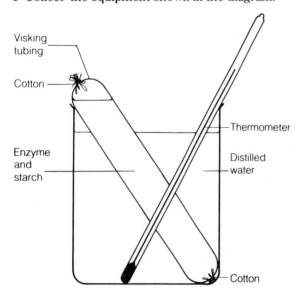

2 In your group design the procedure. You will need to make decisions about a number of points. Here are some of them for you to consider.

- The quantities of starch and enzyme to use.
- The starting temperature of the starch and enzyme before you mix them.
- How and where to mix the reactants.
- The temperature of the water in the beaker.
- How to keep the temperatures steady.
- How and when to carry out tests for the presence of starch and glucose in the distilled water.
- The results you need to record.

Hints:
- Have a clear idea about the procedure by writing out the sequence of tasks to be done.
- Share out these tasks before you start.
- Soak the Visking tube in water before trying to open it out.

Results

Design a table for your results into which you can write the time, and the results of the glucose and starch tests.

Discussion

1 Think of a way to present the results in graph form.

2 Describe any patterns that the graphs show.

3 In your group agree on an explanation of those patterns and the relationship between them.

4 Do your results agree with the theory you started out with? If not, describe the changes you need to make either to your theory or to the procedure.

5 Now write a full report of your theory, the procedure you designed, your results, patterns and graphs and an account of your findings.

6 In what ways is this model unrealistic in its attempt to represent the human digestive system?

7 An enzyme is often described as a 'biological catalyst'. What do you think this means?

8 Make a list of other enzymes found in the human digestive system and write down what they do.

Attainment
Target 3
**PROCESSES
OF LIFE**

Level 9

PRACTICAL 5

Photosynthesis

The productivity of an ecosystem depends on the photosynthetic activity of the plants in it. This in turn depends on various environmental factors which can influence the growth rate of crop plants.

In this experiment you are going to investigate the effect of three such factors on the photosynthetic activity of Canadian pondweed (*Elodea*).

The three factors are:
1 light intensity
2 colour
3 the concentration of carbon dioxide gas.

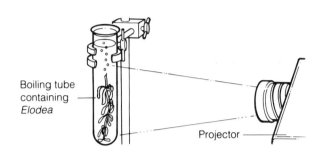

Boiling tube containing *Elodea*

Projector

Equipment

- □ light source, e.g. projector
- □ boiling tube
- □ 100 cm³ measuring cylinder
- □ pondweed (*Elodea*)
- □ stop clock
- □ coloured transparencies
- □ 5 cm³ syringe
- □ 5% sodium bicarbonate solution

Prediction

For each factor predict what you think will happen under the following conditions.

1 The light intensity is varied by gradually decreasing the distance between the plant and the light source.

2 The distance between the plant and light source is fixed but the colour of the transparency put in front of it is changed.

3 The distance between the plant and light source is fixed but the carbon dioxide concentration is varied by the addition of 5 cm³ volumes of 5% sodium bicarbonate solution.

Procedure

1 Use the diagram of the equipment to give you an idea of how to carry out the investigation.
2 The rate of photosynthesis is measured as the rate of production of bubbles of oxygen from the cut stem of the water plant.

3 Count the number of bubbles for a period of 20 seconds at the end of each minute. Multiply this number by three to get rate of bubble formation (bubbles per minute).
Note: living material has a habit of not behaving in a predictable fashion, so be prepared to revise the method of recording in the light of your experience.

Results

Design a table for the data you have collected.

Presentation

Plot graphs of the rate of photosynthesis (in bubbles per minute) against each variable being tested.

Discussion

1 Study the results, looking for patterns or trends. Compare them with your predictions.

2 Write down any conclusions which you think can be based on your results.

3 Attempt to explain the results based on your knowledge of photosynthesis.

4 If your results produce no obvious patterns or trends, or lead to no conclusions, decide whether the experiments need to be repeated because of the way you carried them out.

5 Suggest improvements or refinements to the investigations.

6 Suggest possible applications of the knowledge gained by investigations into the photosynthetic activity of water plants.

ESSENTIAL SCIENCE ACTIVITIES   © K. Bishop, W. Scott, D. Maddocks, 1990

Attainment
Target 3
**PROCESSES
OF LIFE**

Level 7

PRACTICAL 6

Sensory Games (1) – Sight

Blind spot

1 Cover your left eye.
2 Hold this paper about 20 cm away and look at the cross with your right eye.

3 Slowly move the paper back and forth until the spot disappears.
4 Turn the paper upside down and repeat the experiment with the left eye.
5 Explain why the spot disappears.
6 Move the paper from side to side keeping it the same distance away from your eye looking at the cross.
7 What happens to the spot?

Colour blindness

Look through a book of Ishihara colour blindness cards.
1 Did you find any of the cards difficult?
2 Are there any colours which you confuse with one another?
3 Find out what cases colour blindness.

Stereo vision

1 Cover one eye with a blindfold or patch.

2 Try to make the points of two pencils touch.
3 Try it with the other eye covered.
4 Repeat these tests.
5 Describe what happened in each case and try to explain it.

Stereo and peripheral vision

1 On a large piece of paper (for example, A3) draw the rays you would see on a protractor (see diagram).

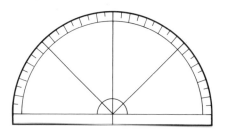

2 Put the paper at the edge of a table and crouch down with your nose at the central position.
3 Ask your partner to stand directly opposite you holding a pencil at the same level as the table.
4 Close your left eye.
5 Look straight ahead and ask your partner to move the pencil gradually to the left.
6 Do not move your eyes to follow it.
7 Tell your partner when the pencil moves out of vision, and write down the angle (A).
8 Now ask your partner to move the pencil to the right and note when it disappears once more (B).
9 Repeat with the right eye closed (C and D).

You will now have four readings (label them A, B, C and D on the diagram). The difference between readings A and D will give you a measure of your peripheral vision – that is, how far you can see out of the corner of your eye. Repeat the experiment for your partner.

Discussion

1 In what situations is this peripheral vision important (that is, when do you need to see out of the corner of your eye?)

2 The difference between the readings B and C gives you a measure of your stereo vision. An object between these two points will be seen by both eyes. This allows you to be able to estimate distances accurately. In what situations is stereo vision important (that is, why do you need to estimate distances accurately)?

3 Make a list of those animals you would expect to have excellent peripheral vision, and another list of animals you would expect to have excellent stereo vision. Explain how you have decided which list to put each animal on.

PRACTICAL 7
Sensory Games (2) – Hearing

Hearing range

1 Listen to a signal generator connected to a loudspeaker.

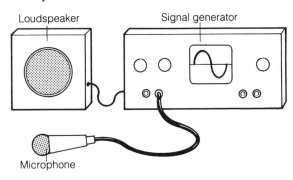

2 Find out the lowest and highest frequencies that your ears can detect These are your threshold levels for the lowest and highest sounds you can hear.

3 Feed the sound into a microphone connected to a cathode ray oscilloscope (CRO).

4 Draw the pattern generated on the CRO for a
  (a) low frequency – about 30 kHz
  (b) middle range frequency – about 5000 kHz
  (c) high frequency – about 15 000 kHz.

5 How does changing the volume of each signal affect the pattern generated on the CRO? Draw a diagram to show the difference.

6 Try your own voice through the microphone. Do you get a simple or complicated pattern on the CRO?

7 Try singing or whistling just one note. Draw a diagram of the waveform of your voice singing that note.

8 If you have musicians amongst you, try some musical instruments. For instance, compare the pattern generated by the note A when produced on a wind instrument such as a flute or clarinet, and when it is produced on a violin.

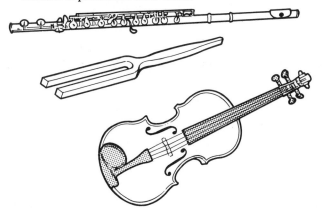

9 Compare these with tuning forks of the same note. Draw diagrams of the waveforms.

10 Explain why the waveforms for different musical instruments and tuning forks playing the same note are different.

Stereo hearing

A baby should respond to sounds made behind its head. It automatically looks behind to see what is going on, but how does it decide which way to turn its head?

The idea in this test is to investigate how our ears locate the source of sound. You will need four filter funnels and two long pieces of rubber tubing. Work in pairs. Look at the picture and arrange the apparatus and yourselves in the same way.

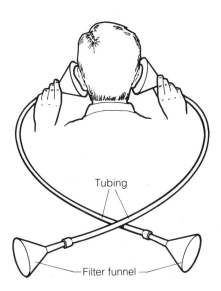

By making soft sounds into the filter funnels, and by crossing the tubes, the listener cannot always be sure where the sound is really coming from. Use this to design a test to investigate how good our ears are at locating the source of a sound.

Describe the experiences you had in this investigation. What have you learnt about how effective our ears are?

Attainment
Target 3
**PROCESSES
OF LIFE**

Level 7

PRACTICAL 8

Sensory Games (3) – Touch

Sensitivity test

Make the apparatus shown in the diagram and design an experiment to investigate the distribution of nerve endings on your fingers, palm and forearm. Work in pairs.

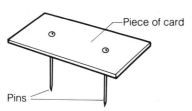

1 Draw a 'map' of the area of skin you want to test.
2 Touch your partner's skin lightly with the pins. Only touch lightly with the pins, otherwise it will not be a fair test. You are investigating touch, not pain!
3 Your partner should say whether two, one or no points are felt.
4 Record your results on your map.
5 Make sure you test the area of skin evenly.
6 The most sensitive areas of the skin will be able to detect both pins each time. Explain why this occurs.
7 Repeat the experiment with the two pins brought closer together. What difference does this make to your map?

Distinguishing surfaces

You must be blindfolded. Your partner will place a variety of surfaces in front of you which you have to identify by feel. Complete the table by putting a tick for a correct identification and a cross for an incorrect identification.

Surfaces	Skin surfaces			
	knee	forearm	back of hand	fingertips
Velvet Cardboard Carpet Wood Metal Plastic				

Temperature test (1)

1 Put a finger from one hand in beaker 1, and a finger from the other hand in beaker 3 and leave them for a minute. Then put both fingers into beaker 2.

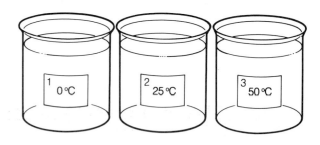

2 Describe what you feel. Are your fingers sensing exact temperatures, or are they sensing differences in temperature?
3 Using your experience from this test explain the following problem.

Two people decide to go swimming. Just before they jump in the pool, Jack has a cold shower and Jenny has a hot shower. How will Jack and Jenny describe the temperature of the pool when they jump in? How will they describe it 5 minutes later?

Temperature test (2)

1 Prepare a range of beakers containing water at different temperatures.
2 Whilst blindfolded, organise the beakers in the order of coldest to hottest using only your fingertips to judge.
3 Make an estimate of the temperature of each beaker of water. Your partner can check your accuracy by using a thermometer.
4 Did you use the same finger each time? Do you think this would make a difference? Explain why the nerve endings in different parts of the skin can become confused about the temperature of the same liquid.

PRACTICAL 9
Sensory Games (4)
– Taste and Smell

It is said that the senses of sight and smell affect the sense of taste.

Crisp test

1 Blindfold your partner.
2 Set out a line of petri dishes containing crisps with different flavours.
3 Draw a sketch of the layout.
4 Ask your partner to hold her/his nose and to try a small part of each crisp in turn.
5 Record what they think the flavours are.
6 Rearrange the order and repeat the test with your partner free to breathe normally.
7 Record these answers.
8 Rearrange the order again.
9 Remove the blindfold and repeat the test.
10 Record the answers.
11 Draw up a table of results and look for patterns. Are there any differences in the ability to identify the tastes correctly?
12 Swap roles, record a second set of results and compare them with the first.

Sugar and salt test

You will need the following solutions in clean cups:

Salt	10%	5%	2%	1%	0.5%	0.1%
Sugar	10%	8%	6%	4%	2%	1%

1 Ask your partner to blindfold you and offer you the solutions in random order.
2 Sip each one; is it salt, sugar or no taste?
3 Between each taste swill your mouth with ordinary water.
4 Your responses should be recorded in a table.
5 Find the threshold level, i.e. the level at which you can just taste the salt or sugar, for each of the tastes.
6 Swap roles, record a second set of responses and compare them with the first set.

Butter and margarine tests

There are many types of butter and margarine on the market. Generally margarine is cheaper but many people say they prefer the taste of butter.

Margarine manufacturers claim that many margarines do taste like butter and people cannot taste the difference.

Design an experiment which tests whether or not people in your group can tell the difference.
Here are some guidelines:
1 Decide how many samples of butter and margarine you will use.
2 Decide which brands to use. Remember that you can buy both salted and unsalted butters, hard and soft margarines, and that they have different appearances and smells.
3 Decide whether the butter or margarine will be tasted on its own or on a biscuit.
4 Decide whether the subjects should be able to see what they are eating.

Coca-Cola test

Do supermarket colas taste like Coke or Pepsi, or do you think there is no comparison?

They are certainly a lot cheaper and if you cannot tell the difference why buy the more expensive brands? You will only be paying for the advertising campaigns.

Design a taste test using drinks such as Coca-Cola, Pepsi Cola and supermarket colas to find out if you think there really is a difference in taste.

Attainment
Target 3
**PROCESSES
OF LIFE**

Level 7

PRACTICAL 10

Growth of Plants

Plants are called producers because they can manufacture their own food from CO_2 and H_2O by photosynthesis. However, to grow successfully they also need other nutrients which they obtain through their roots.

In this experiment you will investigate the need for nitrogen, phosphorus and potassium in a small floating duckweed called *Lemna*. The growth of *Lemna* can easily be measured by counting the number of new plants.

Design

Work in small groups. Choose the equipment from the list below and any other that is available, and design an experiment that will test the need of *Lemna* for nitrogen, potassium and phosphorus.

Discuss your ideas with the others in your group and agree on an experimental design.

Make sure you have a control experiment, and that you control all other variables, such as temperature and light.

Equipment

- □ selection of culture solutions labelled 'nitrogen deficient' 'phosphorus deficient' 'potassium deficient' 'full culture'
- □ petri dishes
- □ pipettes
- □ measuring cylinder
- □ *Lemna* plants

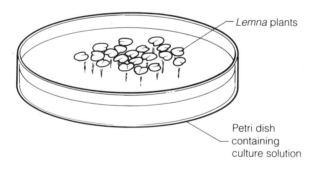

Lemna plants

Petri dish containing culture solution

Results

Design a table for your results.

Collect data over a period of time long enough for any differences in growth to appear.

Presentation

Plot a graph showing the increase in the number of *Lemna* plants against time for each culture solution.

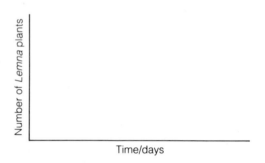

Number of *Lemna* plants

Time/days

Discussion

1 Write down your conclusions about which nutrients the duckweed *Lemna* needs.

2 Are your results similar to those of other groups? If not, suggest reasons for the differences?

3 Why might farmers be interested in the results of such experiments?

4 Farmers who rotate their crops often include clover; whereas farmers who grow only one crop use large amounts of fertiliser. On the basis of your results, suggest reasons why they do this.

5 It is claimed that a reduction in growth could be reversed by transferring the *Lemna* plants to a full culture solution. Design an experiment to test this idea.

Attainment
Target 3
**PROCESSES
OF LIFE**

Level 9

PRACTICAL 11

Separating Colours in Plants

Plants appear green because they reflect the green part of light and absorb other colours – as this graph shows:

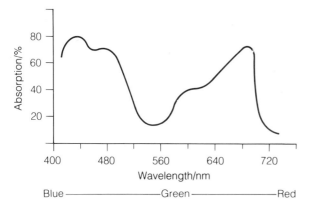

Absorption spectrum for chlorophyll

But are there other colours besides green in the plant material? In this experiment you are going to use paper chromatography to investigate this.

Equipment

- pestle and mortar
- silver sand
- pin
- boiling tube
- bung fitted with hook
- chromatography paper
- solvent (9:1 petroleum ether: acetone)
- nettle or spinach leaves

Procedure

1 Cut off a few young nettle leaves from the tip of a nettle plant (in winter you could use frozen spinach).
2 Grind the leaves up with a pestle and mortar with a small amount of solvent and some fine silver sand. Continue until you have a dark green extract.
3 Pour the liquid portion of the extract into a centrifuge tube and spin it for two minutes.
4 Cut a piece of chromatography paper so that it will fit neatly into a boiling tube.
5 Draw a pencil line across the paper 1 cm from the end that will be in the solvent. Mark the centre of the line with a dot.
6 Very carefully, use the head of a pin to transfer tiny amounts of the green extract to the spot you have just marked on the paper. Repeat this many times until you have built up a concentrated dark spot. Do not let it get too big by trying to transfer too much at a time.

7 Put some solvent in the boiling tube. Hang the paper in the boiling tube so that the green spot is well above the level of the solvent but the filter paper just dips into the solvent.

8 Wait until the solvent runs up the paper to just below the hook. Then take the paper out of the boiling tube and let it dry.

Results

With a pencil, mark the point that the solvent reached, and the points at which you can see any different colours. Measure these distances and record them along with their colours.

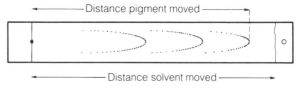

Discussion

1 Describe your chromatogram. How many different coloured pigments are found in chlorophyll?

2 From the measurements that you have made it is possible to identify the different pigments by calculating their R_f values.

$$R_f = \frac{\text{distance of pigment from baseline}}{\text{distance solvent moved from baseline}}$$

Draw up a table of colours and their R_f values. Collect the results obtained by other groups and tabulate them. What do you notice about them.

3 Compare your results with the graph to see if there is a link. Why do you think plants might need more than one pigment?

4 Predict whether all plants will have exactly the same pigments. Choose another plant and repeat the experiment to see if your prediction is supported.

Attainment
Target 3
**PROCESSES
OF LIFE**

Level 5

PRACTICAL 12

Investigating Water in Food

All fresh food contains water. Meat, like the human body, is about 70 per cent water, and plants contain even more – lettuce is about 95 per cent water. Some food manufacturers use polyphosphates to hold water in their food. You can pay for extra water in this way.

In this experiment you will investigate the percentage of water in a variety of foods. One way of doing this is to rehydrate some commercial dehydrated foods. Examples of such foods are dried peas, carrots, onions and TVP (textured vegetable protein).

Equipment

☐ 150 cm³ beaker

☐ scraps of paper

☐ electric balance

☐ selection of dehydrated foods

Procedure

1 Set up a beaker containing 100 cm³ of water on a tripod and gauze over a Bunsen burner.
2 While the water comes to the boil, measure out about 10 g of one of the dehydrated foods. Write down the exact mass of this sample.
3 Add the sample to the water and simmer it gently until the food seems to be fully rehydrated.
4 Drain and remove excess water from the food.
5 Measure the new mass of the food.
6 Copy and fill in this table.
7 Repeat the experiment for the other foods.

Results

Record your results in a table as shown below:

Food	Original mass M1	Mass after rehydration M2	Percentage of water in food $\dfrac{M2 - M1}{M2} \times 100\%$

Calculation using a calculator of percentage of water in a food:

- Key in M2
- Key in M1
- Key in M2
- Key in 100

- Press –
- Press ÷
- Press ×
- Press =

Your answer should lie between 0 and 100%. Round it to the nearest whole number.

Discussion

1 Write down the average percentage of water in each of the foods you tested. List them in rank order, highest percentage first, and then draw a stacked block graph.

2 Was there any pattern in the results between the type of food and the amount of water it absorbed.

3 Why did you drain the rehydrated foods before reweighing them?

4 Collect results from other groups that used the same foods as you did and draw up a table to compare them. Are the results similar? If not can you find reasons to explain the difference?

5 Rehydrating already dehydrated foods is not the best way of finding the percentage of water. Explain what the disadvantages are, and why it would be better to dehydrate fresh food in order to calculate the percentage of water it contains.

6 Make a list of the foods found in a supermarket which contain dehydrated ingredients. Why do you think food is dehydrated commercially?

7 Whilst in the supermarket try to make a list of those foods which contain phosphates or polyphosphates.

8 Mountaineers take lots of dehydrated foods on their expeditions. There are two main reasons for taking this type of food. What are they?

9 Nutritionists would advise against consuming too much dehydrated food. What are they concerned about?

ESSENTIAL SCIENCE ACTIVITIES   © K. Bishop, W. Scott, D. Maddocks, 1990

Attainment
Target 3
**PROCESSES
OF LIFE**

Level 5

PRACTICAL 13

Investigating Vitamin C

Green leafy vegetables such as cabbage, and citrus fruits such as grapefruit and oranges are high in vitamin C. The vitamin C content of a food is easy to monitor and is a good indicator of nutritional quality. Over-processed or overcooked food can easily be detected by measuring the loss in vitamin C.

In this experiment you will investigate the vitamin C content of a selection of fruit juices.

Equipment

- four 150 cm³ conical flasks
- 10 cm³ pipette
- 50 cm³ burette
- blue DCPIP dye

Procedure

1 Decide which fruit juices you are going to test.
2 Set up the apparatus as shown in the diagram.

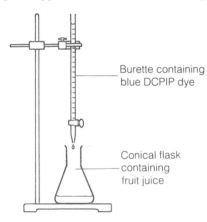

Burette containing
blue DCPIP dye

Conical flask
containing
fruit juice

3 Pipette 10 cm³ of fruit juice into the conical flask.
4 Fill the burette to the 0.0 cm³ mark with the blue dye (see diagram).

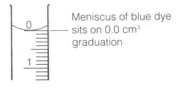

Meniscus of blue dye
sits on 0.0 cm³
graduation

5 Very slowly, let the blue dye into the conical flask (about 1 cm³ at a time).
6 Close the tap and swirl the flask gently to disperse the dye.
7 When you see a faint pink colour which cannot be swirled away, make a note of the amount of dye used.
8 Repeat the titration accurately twice more.

Results

Draw up a results table with the headings as shown below. Calculate the average value for the three titrations.

Type of fruit juice	Titration 1 (cm³)	Titration 2 (cm³)	Titration 3 (cm³)	Average (cm³)

The amount of DCPIP (dichlorophenolindolphenol) dye used indicated the vitamin C content of the fruit juice. Your teacher will provide you with the figure to convert the amount of dye into mg of vitamin C per litre of fruit juice.

Discussion

1 Collect and tabulate the results from the whole class putting them in rank order from high vitamin C content to low vitamin C content.

2 Repeat the experiment using fruit juices which claim to have a high vitamin C content.

3 Is there a link between the price of the fruit juice and the vitamin C content?

4 It is known that high temperatures will break down the vitamin C. Design an experiment which could investigate the effect of heat on the breakdown of vitamin C in a fruit juice.

5 It is said that the region just under the skin of a potato has a much higher level of vitamin C than deeper inside. Design an experiment to test this idea.

Attainment
Target 5
**HUMAN
INFLUENCES
ON THE EARTH**
Level 8

PRACTICAL 14
Clean Air from Power Stations

There is great concern about air pollution across Europe. Power stations are a major source of this pollution. This is because the coal and oil which they burn contains sulphur. When this burns, it produces sulphur dioxide gas (SO_2) which escapes from the power station through the chimney. Oxides of nitrogen are also produced in power stations. These gases then either fall to the ground in the surrounding countryside or are carried on winds for many miles to other countries and continents.

In the air, the sulphur dioxide can react with oxygen and water to form sulphuric acid, and the nitrogen oxides form nitric acid in the air. These acids are then washed to the earth in the rain.

Rain water is naturally acidic – because of the carbon dioxide which is dissolved in it. Its pH should be around 5.6. Often, however, rain water has a pH of below 4, and the most acidic rain recorded in the UK was at Pitlochry in Scotland – a pH of 2.4.

There are several ways of reducing this problem:
- using cleaner fuels
- using less fuel
- cleaning the gases before release
- using less electricity
- changing the way the fuel is burnt.

Each of these has something to offer in the fight against pollution. In this investigation, you will look at the last of the methods listed.

In power stations, it is possible to mix the coal with chemicals which will absorb the sulphur dioxide which is produced. One of the best chemicals for this is calcium carbonate because it is readily available and cheap.

Equipment

- test tubes, stands, clamps
- Bunsens
- glass tubing
- filter paper and indicator solution

Design

Using the apparatus listed – and any other you need – design an investigation to compare burning coal on its own and a mixture of coal and limestone.

You can test for the presence of sulphur dioxide by using a solution of potassium dichromate – or dichromate indicator paper. This turns from orange to green when exposed to sulphur dioxide.

Plan your investigation, and then get your teacher's approval before you begin.

Results

Write a few lines about your investigation. Say what you did, and what you discovered. Include a sketch of your apparatus.

Discussion

1 Write a chemical equation for the burning of sulphur in air to produce sulphur dioxide.

2 If some coal contains 1 per cent sulphur, and 1000 kg of the coal is completely burnt, how much sulphur dioxide will be produced.

3 Write a chemical equation for the reaction of sulphur dioxide, oxygen and water in the atmosphere to form sulphuric acid (H_2SO_4).

4 pH is measured on a log scale. If the pH increases by 1 unit, the acidity decreases 10 times. The lower the pH, the more acidic is the water.
  (a) How many times more acidic is rain with a pH of 4 than rain with a pH of 5?
  (b) How many times more acidic is rain with a pH of 4.5 than rain with a pH of 5.5?

ESSENTIAL SCIENCE ACTIVITIES   © K. Bishop, W. Scott, D. Maddocks, 1990

Attainment
Target 5
**HUMAN
INFLUENCES
ON THE EARTH**
Level 7

PRACTICAL 15

Treading on Grass

It is clear that the activity of human beings can have a significant impact on the global environment. It is also possible to see examples of how human activity can have much smaller environmental effects.

You need to find an area of grassy land crossed by unofficial footpaths where human activity has worn the grass down, but not made it bare.

The purpose of the investigation is to see whether human activity has an effect on the species and distribution of the plants that grow there.

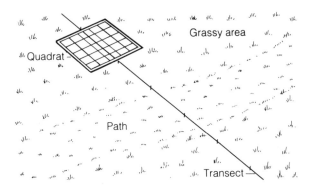

Once you have decided on the area you are going to study you must either identify all the plants that grow there or give each species a number.

Equipment

☐ string

☐ metre rule

☐ 0.5 m square quadrat

☐ wooden stakes

Procedure

1 Make a list of all the plants that exist in the grassy area. Either identify them or sketch and number each type.
2 Stretch the string across and at right angles to the path.
3 Put the quadrat down at one end and estimate the percentage area in the quadrat covered by each type of plant. Record the figures in a table.
4 Pick up the quadrat, move it on 0.5 m and record the estimated percentages in your results table. Repeat the estimations at 0.5 m intervals along the length of the transect.

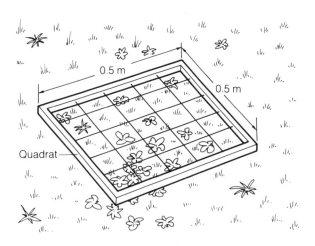

Presentation

Present your results as kite diagrams — one above the other as shown here.
Mark the position of the path.

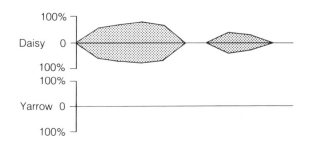

Discussion

1 What assumption do you have to make about the distribution of plants before human activity created a path?

2 Describe how the pattern of plants changes along the length of the transect.

3 Can you draw any conclusions about the effect of humans on the distribution of the plants.

4 Try to think of reasons which could explain why some plants cannot survive in the path region.

5 Suggest ways of extending this investigation.

Attainment
Target 6
**TYPES AND
USES OF
MATERIALS**

PRACTICAL 16

Displacement Reactions

Knowing something about how reactive a metal is, means you may be able to predict whether chemical reactions will take place or not. The reactivity order of a number of different metals is given below:

1 magnesium
2 zinc
3 aluminium
4 iron
5 lead
6 copper

The theory is that the more reactive a metal is, the more likely it is to displace the metal in another compound. The equation for a reaction can be written like this:

metal A + B oxide → metal B + A oxide

In this case, metal A is more reactive than metal B.

Prediction

The table shows a series of reactions where the metals listed above are added to solutions of other metal salts.

Complete the table. With a tick or a cross predict for each combination of metal and solution whether a reaction is expected or not. Then test your predictions experimentally.

Equipment

- test tubes
- test tube rack
- pair of tweezers
- plastic ruler
- metals
- metal salt solutions

Procedure

1 Plan the order in which you will carry out all the tests, and decide how you will make the reaction happen as quickly as possible.
2 Think about how you will know whether a reaction has taken place or not.
3 Put 2 cm depth of metal salt solution into a test tube.
4 Add one of the metals.
5 Decide whether there is a reaction or not.
6 Record the test in your results table by putting in another tick or cross next to the one that is already there.
7 Wash out the metal salt solution and dispose of it safely. Do not get any of the chemicals on your hands.
8 Complete the set of reactions.

Discussion

1 Compare your results with the set of predictions you made earlier.

2 What differences were there between your results and your predictions? Try to explain any differences. Were there problems in deciding whether there was a reaction or not?

3 If you are unsure about any of the results, check the reactions again.

4 How do they compare now?

5 Would you make any modifications to the reactivity series shown on this paper?

Metal \ Salt	Lead nitrate	Magnesium sulphate	Iron (II) sulphate	Aluminium sulphate	Zinc sulphate	Copper sulphate
lead						
magnesium						
iron						
aluminium						
zinc						
copper						

Attainment
Target 6
**TYPES AND
USES OF
MATERIALS**
Level 8

PRACTICAL 17

Packets of Milk

Milk is sold in glass bottles, and in cartons. In 1987, 5 900 million litres of milk were sold in the UK, and an increasing amount of this is ultra heat treated (UHT) milk.

To make UHT milk, the first thing that has to happen is that the fat layer and the water layer are completely mixed. This is done by forcing warm milk through small holes.

Then, the temperature of the milk is raised to about 140 °C for a very short time. This kills dangerous organisms in the milk. This can happen in different ways: steam is sprayed into the milk or milk is sprayed into steam.

This UHT milk is now sterile. To make sure that no micro-organisms get into it, it has to be put into the cartons with great care. This process is called aseptic packaging. The milk is kept away from the air, and the packaging material is sterilised.

The full cartons of milk have to be sterile, completely sealed and strong. They also have to stop light reaching the milk.

One of the advantages of UHT milk is that micro-organisms are completely destroyed but the flavour of the milk is only affected a little. This means that the milk can be stored unrefrigerated for a long time.

In these investigations, you will look at the material which is used in UHT milk cartons, and see how strong it is.

Equipment

- ☐ empty cartons of UHT milk
- ☐ ordinary lab equipment
- ☐ scissors

Procedure

1 Cut open an empty carton of UHT milk. How many layers does the material seem to have? Try to identify what each of the layers is made of, and suggest a reason why each layer is used.

2 One reason for having several layers – this is called a laminated structure – is to provide strength. But what happens if one of the layers is taken away? Cut two rectangles from the material (each should be about 5 cm × 3 cm). Remove the inside layer from one of them. You will need to do this with care.

Now think of a way of finding out how much force is needed to tear each of the pieces. Remember it has to be a fair comparison. Talk to your teacher when you have a plan.

Results

Make a display of your results. This should include an explanation of the method which you used, and should show your results clearly.

Discussion

1 Milk is not the only food which is kept in this kind of packaging. Have a look at home – and the next time you go shopping – to see what other foods you can find packaged in this way.

2 How many other laminated structures can you think of? Are they used for strength – or are there other reasons?

3 There are two other common ways of treating milk to remove unwanted micro-organisms. One is pasteurisation. The other is sterilisation. Find out as much as you can about these processes, and how they differ from ultra heat treatment.

Attainment
Target 6
**TYPES AND
USES OF
MATERIALS**
Level 8

PRACTICAL 18

Investigating Tea-bags

More than 160 000 tonnes of tea is sold in the UK each year. 78 per cent of that is in the form of tea-bags. The early tea-bags were made from muslin – a fine cotton cloth. These were expensive because the muslin had to be stitched. Today's tea-bag cloth is very different. It is made of a mixture of these things.

- Wood pulp – This is made from trees and is also used to make paper.
- Abaca hemp – This is the fibrous layer inside the bark of the abaca tree. Ropes and twine can be made from this.
- Polypropylene – This is a synthetic fibre which is made from petroleum. Polypropylene is also used to make carpets, ropes, string, packaging materials, plastic films, etc.

Wood pulp and hemp provide lightness and strength; polypropylene fibres melt when they are heated – forming the seal round the edge of the tea-bag.

The following investigations look at the structure and strength of tea-bags.

Equipment

- ☐ microscope or hand lens
- ☐ fresh tea-bags
- ☐ ordinary lab equipment

Procedure

1 The structure of a tea-bag is important. The material has to let water mix with the tea leaves, and allow the tea solution to escape. While this is happening, the bag must remain in one piece.

Take an unused tea-bag and cut one edge. Empty the tea into a waste-paper basket.

Hold the material against the light; sketch what you see. Now use a hand lens or a low-power microscope and look at the structure of the fabric. Make a drawing of this.

From what you have seen, do you think that the material will have the same strength in all directions? Give your reasons.

2 Now think of an experiment which will let you test your ideas about the strength of the fabric. You should use ordinary lab equipment to find out how much force is needed to tear the fabric in different directions.

When you know what you want to do, talk to your teacher so that your plan can be approved.

3 Of course, it is the strength of tea-bags when they are hot and wet that matters. Think of a way of carrying out your investigation to find out if the strength of the material is different when it is wet.

Results

Now look at all your results and make a report to the rest of the group on what you have found. You might use a poster or a written report – whichever you think is best.

Discussion

1 It is now possible to buy tea bags which are round rather than square. Can you see any advantage in the round ones?

2 Which kind of tea-bag do you think uses the least material?

ESSENTIAL SCIENCE ACTIVITIES © K. Bishop, W. Scott, D. Maddocks, 1990

PRACTICAL 19
Salt and the Enzyme in Saliva

Salivary amylase is an enzyme that catalyses (speeds up) the breakdown of large molecules of starch into smaller molecules of glucose. It is thought that there are factors in the mouth and in food which affect the activity of this enzyme. One of these factors is the amount of salt present.

In this experiment you are going to investigate the activity of the enzyme in a series of different concentrations of salt. The progress of the reaction is tested with iodine solution. When all the starch is broken down the iodine no longer turns black.

Equipment

- the following concentrations of salt: 0.01%, 0.04%, 0.08%, 0.10%, 0.14%
- distilled water
- 1% starch solution
- amylase
- water bath at 37 °C
- test tubes and test tube rack
- labels
- spotting tile
- iodine solution
- stop clock

Procedure

1 Have a water bath prepared at 37 °C (body temperature).
2 Label six test tubes 1 – 6. Stick the labels near the mouth of the test tube. Prepare them as shown in the table.

1	2	3	4	5	6
1 cm³ dist. water	1 cm³ 0.01% salt	1 cm³ 0.04% salt	1 cm³ 0.08% salt	1 cm³ 0.10% salt	1 cm³ 0.14% salt
10 cm³ 1% starch	10 cm³ 1% starch	10 cm³ 1% starch	10 cm³ 1% starch	10 cm³ 1% starch	10 cm³ 1% starch

3 Leave the tubes in the water bath for 10 minutes, but do not let the labels get wet.

4 Collect another six test tubes and put 2 cm³ of enzyme (amylase) into each and put them in the same water bath.
5 Prepare a spotting tile by putting drops of iodine solution into the depressions.
6 When the ten minutes is up, quickly add 2 cm³ of enzyme into each of the numbered tubes. Set the clock running and leave it. Do not stop it until the experiment is over.
7 After 1 minute, transfer 1 drop of the reaction mixture from tube 1 onto the first drop of iodine in row 1 of the tile. Repeat with the other tubes.
8 Set out a new row of iodine drops. Repeat the test at regular intervals – every two minutes or so. Important – record the exact time that each tube requires for the iodine to give a negative test, that is, no more black colour.

Results

Design a table which will allow you to record the tube number and the time it took before there was no longer a positive test for starch.

Presentation

Plot a graph of the rate of reaction (1/time) against the salt concentration (%).

Discussion

1 Describe the shape of the graph and say what happens to the rate of reaction as the salt concentration increases from 0% to 0.14%.

2 If you see a pattern in your results explain what effect you think the salt is having on the activity of the enzyme.

3 Write down any relevance or practical use for your results.

4 List any other factors which you think might either increase or decrease the activity of the enzyme.

PRACTICAL 20
The Effect of Enzymes on Proteins

Protein foods are an important part of our diet. We need protein for the growth and repair of body tissues. Proteins are made from amino acids. These are often called the 'building blocks' of life because we obtain them from our food and then use them to make our own proteins.

Proteins are broken down in our digestive system, particularly in the stomach and the small intestine. Enzymes are important in this process.

The purpose of this experiment is to investigate the action of the enzyme pepsin on the protein egg white.

Equipment

□ test tubes

□ test tube rack

□ egg white solution

□ pepsin (enzyme) solution

□ boiled pepsin solution

□ dilute hydrochloric acid solution

□ distilled water

□ water bath set at 37 °C

□ thermometer

□ 250 cm³ beaker

Prediction

You are going to set up the tubes as shown in the table below. Before you start predict an order for the sequence in which the tubes turn from cloudy to clear. Becoming clear shows that the protein is being broken down. Use your knowledge of enzymes, the conditions they prefer and the human digestive system to make your prediction.

	A	B	C	D
egg-white	2cm³	2cm³	2cm³	2cm³
1% pepsin	1cm³	-	1cm³	-
hydrochloric acid	-	3 drops	3 drops	3 drops
boiled pepsin	-	-	-	1cm³
distilled water	3 drops	1cm³	-	-

Procedure

1 Set up the tubes as described in the table.
2 Have ready a water bath (beaker of water over a Bunsen) ready at 37 °C.
3 Place the test tubes in the water bath. Do not let the temperature get above 40 °C. Watch carefully for 15 minutes.
4 Record the order in which the contents of the tubes go from cloudy to clear.

Discussion

1 Compare your results with your prediction. Explain any differences you find.

2 In which part of the body would you expect to find pepsin.

3 Pepsin is a protease – it breaks proteins down. Find out the names of some other proteases and where they can be found in the human body.

4 These graphs show the activity of the pepsin. Use them to explain the relationship of the activity of pepsin with pH and temperature.

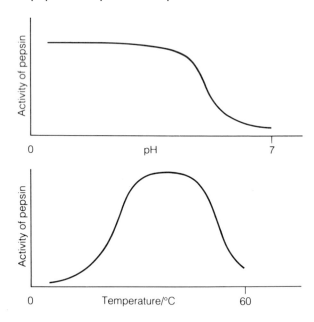

Attainment
Target 7
**MAKING NEW
MATERIALS**

Level 8

PRACTICAL 21

Reaction and Concentration

How does concentration affect the speed of a chemical reaction? Common sense tells you that if particles are crowded together they are more likely to collide and react.

In this experiment you are going to test this idea and see if there is a link between the time it takes for a reaction to happen (i.e. the rate), and the concentration of the chemicals. The reaction is:

sodium + hydrochloric → sulphur
thiosulphate acid

The sulphur appears as a yellow cloud and sinks to the bottom as a precipitate.

Equipment

- □ 150 cm³ beaker
- □ stop clock
- □ 100 cm³ measuring cylinders
- □ dilute hydrochloric acid
- □ sodium thiosulphate solution
- □ distilled water

Prediction

Write a sentence which predicts what will happen to the rate of reaction as the concentration of sodium thiosulphate is increased.

Procedure

Design a series of experiments so that the concentration of sodium thiosulphate reacting with the acid is gradually increased. Use the following points to help you:
- ● the total reaction volume must be the same in each experiment.
- ● the acid and the sodium thiosulphate are both clear solutions. The sulphur makes them cloudy.

Think of a way to decide when the solution is no longer transparent, and use that to mark the end of the reaction.
- ● do a test run to decide how to judge the end point.

Results

Draw a results table using the headings shown here:

Volume (cm³)			Time taken for	Rate
thiosulphate	water	acid	reaction(s)	(1/time)

Presentation

Plot a graph of the rate of reaction (1/time) against the volume of sodium thiosulphate.

Volume of sodium thiosulphate/cm³

Discussion

1 Describe the shape of the graph. How is the rate of reaction linked to the concentration of the sodium thiosulphate.

2 Based on your knowledge of chemical reactions explain the pattern of your results.

Attainment
Target 7
**MAKING NEW
MATERIALS**

Level 7

PRACTICAL 22

Indigestion

Drug companies are keen to get us to buy soluble tablets for headache or indigestion. Apparently they take effect much more quickly if they readily break up into small particles. Some products are actually sold in powder form.

In this experiment you are going to test the idea that the speed that the drug takes to work depends on the size of the particles.

Prediction

What do you think? Make a prediction of how the size of drug particles affects the speed at which it takes effect.

Equipment

- gas syringe
- 250 cm³ conical flask
- 25 cm³ measuring cylinder
- U-tube
- delivery tubes
- rubber bungs and connectors
- stop clock
- cotton wool
- dilute hydrochloric acid
- anti-acid (indigestion) tablets

Procedure

Design a fair test which can compare the effect of different sized particles on the rate of reaction. Keep the following points in mind:
- the equipment is set up as shown in the diagram.

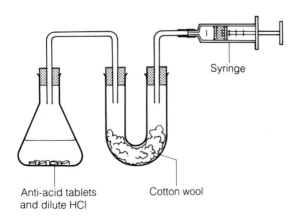

Syringe

Anti-acid tablets
and dilute HCl

Cotton wool

- the indigestion tablets have to be broken up into different sized particles.
- the same mass of anti-acid tablet must be used each time with the same volume of acid.
- the rate of reaction can be measured by recording the volume of CO_2 in the syringe at fixed intervals of time.
- you will need to do some trial runs to find the best concentration for the acid. If the reaction is too fast then the acid must be diluted with distilled water.

Results

Record the volume of carbon dioxide gas in the syringe at fixed intervals of time.

Presentation

On one pair of axes plot the graph of volume of gas produced against time for each size of particle.

Discussion

1 Compare your results with your prediction? Describe the pattern or trend that you see.

2 Write down any conclusions you think you can make based on your results.

3 Give an explanation of your results based on your knowledge of chemical reactions.

4 If there is no obvious pattern to your results decide whether your experiment needs to be redesigned and repeated. If it does, how could you improve the experiment?

5 If possible, use what you have learnt from your results to say whether you think the drug companies are right to make their products in powder or soluble form.

ESSENTIAL SCIENCE ACTIVITIES © K. Bishop, W. Scott, D. Maddocks, 1990

Attainment
Target 7
**MAKING NEW
MATERIALS**

Level 7

PRACTICAL 23

Preserving Food (Part 1)

Recently food poisoning has hit the headlines and seems to be on the increase. It appears to be caused by people not understanding about the conditions in which bacteria grow. The graph shows the effect of temperature on the growth of *Listeria* bacteria.

In this experiment you are going to investigate some methods used to protect food from spoilage. The procedure is outlined in Preserving Food (Part 2).

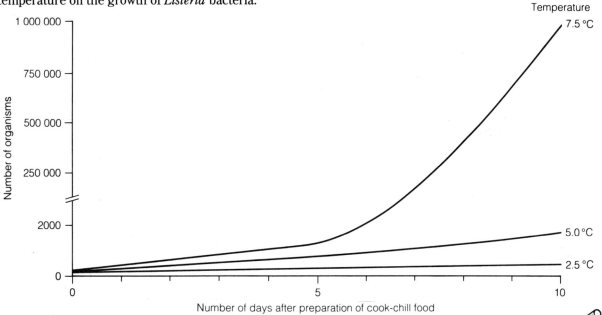

Growth of *Listeria* bacteria in cook-chill foods

The difference temperature makes is quite dramatic, and you can see why foods are stored at low temperatures.

There are also many other ways in which our foods can be protected from the action of microbes and other forms of spoilage. Here is a list of commonly used methods and an example of each:

	Treatment	Example
(a)	heat treatment	baked beans
(b)	freezing	frozen peas
(c)	acid treatment	pickled onions
(d)	salt treatment	salted bacon
(e)	sugar treatment	strawberry jam
(f)	sulphur dioxide treatment	orange squash
(g)	smoking	smoked fish
(h)	dehydration	dried peas
(i)	vacuum or nitrogen packing	cheese, bacon
(j)	nitrate and nitrite salts	cooked meats

Petri dish containing
nutrient agar

Inoculating loop

Equipment

☐ set of nutrient agar petri dishes

☐ pipette

☐ sterile loop

☐ *Bacillus subtilis* culture

☐ antiseptic

☐ weak salt solution

☐ strong salt solution

☐ weak sugar solution

☐ strong sugar solution

☐ sulphur dioxide solution

☐ paper straw

☐ disinfectant

☐ vinegar

☐ bleach

Attainment
Target 7
**MAKING NEW
MATERIALS**

Level 7

PRACTICAL 24

Preserving Food (Part 2)

Procedure

1 Work in small groups. Your teacher will tell you how many nutrient agar plates to use.
2 Inoculate your plates with the bacterium (*Bacillus subtilis*).
(a) Heat your inoculation loop in a Bunsen burner until it glows red. It is now sterile.
(b) Now pass the open mouth of the bottle containing the bacteria quickly through the bunsen flame.
(c) Dip the loop into the bottle and transfer one drop to each agar plate.
(d) Repeat the process several times until there is sufficient liquid to be spread over each plate.
(e) Use the loop to make a criss-cross pattern over the surface of the agar. Do not cut into the agar surface.
3 Treat your agar plates as follows to mimic the methods of food treatment. Pipette the solutions you are adding over the agar as shown in the diagram. Seal with sticky tape to prevent bacteria entering the plates from the air.

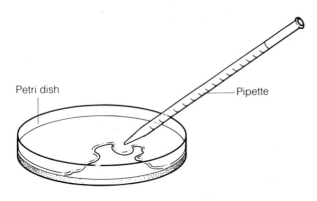

Petri dish — Pipette

Your teacher will tell you which treatments to do.
(a) Seal and put in a steriliser for 15 minutes.
(b) Seal and store in a freezer.
(c) Add 2 cm³ of vinegar and seal.
(d) Add 2 cm³ of strong salt solution and seal.
(e) Add 2 cm³ of weak salt solution and seal.
(f) Add 2 cm³ of strong sugar solution and seal.
(g) Add 2 cm³ of weak sugar solution and seal.
(h) Add 2 cm³ of sulphur dioxide solution and seal.
(i) Light a paper straw and pass the smoke over the agar and then seal.

(j) Add 2 cm³ of antiseptic and seal.
(k) Add 2 cm³ of disinfectant and seal.
(l) Add 2 cm³ of bleach and seal.
(m) Just seal the plate.
4 Apart from (b) all the plates are then stored in an incubator set at 37 °C and left for 24 hours in order to find out if the *Bacillus subtilis* microbes will grow.
5 After 24 hours, describe the appearance of the plates and tabulate the results for the whole class.

Results

Make two lists, one for agar plates on which no bacteria grew and one for plates on which bacteria did grow. Collect information from the rest of the class so you have two complete lists.

Draw a table showing the results from the whole class.

Discussion

1 Try to draw up another list which puts the agar plates in order with the plate showing the greatest amount of bacterial growth at the top and the plate with none or least at the bottom.

2 Which methods of preservation seem to have been the most effective? Make an attempt to explain why they were effective.

3 This experiment used a bacterium called *Bacillus subtilis*. Would you expect to get the same, similar or a different set of results with *Listeria* bacteria, for instance?

4 For each of the food preservation methods explain the principle on which it works, for instance keeping food cool inhibits the reproduction of the bacteria.

5 A supermarket in one of Britain's major cities was found to be storing cook-chill foods at temperatures of 7 to 10 °C. As an Environmental Health Officer what action would you wish to take against the supermarket?

6 Why is it that the growth of the bacteria appears to remain dormant for about three to five days and then suddenly erupts?

PRACTICAL 25
Why do Apples go Brown when Cut?

Some apples and potatoes turn brown once they have been cut. It is the action of enzymes and oxygen which cause this browning. Normally this does not matter if the food is to be cooked or eaten straight away. There are cases, however, when cut fruit or vegetables need to be stored and must be stopped from browning. If the enzymes can be inactivated or oxygen excluded, then browning can be prevented. The following factors are thought to affect the browning process:
- heat
- acid
- vitamin C solution
- low temperature.

In this practical you will design an experiment to study one of these factors.

Design

Work in small groups. Each group should choose only one of the factors to test. Choose equipment from the list, and any other laboratory equipment that is available, and design an experiment which will test the factor you have chosen. Discuss your ideas with the others in your group and agree on a procedure.

Make sure you have a control experiment as well as your test experiment, otherwise you will have nothing to compare your results with.

Equipment

- beakers
- bench acid
- vitamin C solution
- pipettes
- knife
- peeler
- lemon juice
- access to a refrigerator
- measuring cylinder
- electric balance
- several varieties of apples and potatoes

Discussion

1 Write a report on your experiment. In this report you should outline your method and results.

2 Present a brief summary of your findings to the rest of the class outlining how the factor you chose affected the browning of the food.

3 Compare and discuss the results of your experiment with other groups who chose to test the same factor.

4 Potatoes or apples prepared early before being cooked are usually stored temporarily in water. On the basis of your results can you explain the reason for this? What disadvantages are there in this?

5 How would you store peeled potatoes for about an hour? How would you store them for a longer time?

6 It is important for food manufacturers involved in the processing of potatoes and apples fully to understand the browning process. Find out what steps they take to minimise the effects of browning.

Attainment
Target 7
**MAKING NEW
MATERIALS**

Level 7

PRACTICAL 26

Investigating the Freshness of Milk

Most homes today have a refrigerator which means you can keep milk fresh for longer. Usually, freshness is judged by the smell, but this is not necessarily the best method. Two tests which are used to make a more scientific judgement are:

- clotting test – sour milk will clot when heated,
- resazurin test – this blue dye turns pink in sour milk.

The dairies pasteurise milk by passing it through a heat exchanger for 15 seconds at a temperature of 72 °C.

Equipment

- ☐ six test tubes
- ☐ test tube rack
- ☐ water bath, set at 95–8 °C
- ☐ labelled milk samples
- ☐ 5 cm³ syringe
- ☐ resazurin dye

Procedure

You are supplied with four samples of milk. You are going to carry out the two tests on each sample.

Clotting test

1 Put 10 cm³ of each milk sample into labelled test tubes.
2 Put them in a water bath and bring the milk almost to boiling point.
3 Look at the four test tubes. Note the ones where the milk has clotted and smells sour.

Resazurin test

1 Put 5 cm³ of each milk sample into a labelled test tube.
2 Put them into a water bath set at 37 °C and leave them for 10 minutes.
3 Using a syringe, add 1 cm³ of resazurin dye to each test tube. Gently shake the tubes.
4 Record the colour of each tube as soon as the dye has been added. Record the colour every 5 minutes for the next 20 minutes.

Results

Fill in the following table.

Test tube	Clotting test		Resazurin test Colour at 5 minute intervals				
	clotting	smell	0	5	10	15	20
1							
2							
3							
4							

Discussion

1 If milk is fresh it will not clot or smell sour, and the dye will remain blue. If the milk is bad it will clot, smell sour and the dye will change to pink or become colourless. The rate of change of colour of the dye depends on the freshness of the milk. If it is really bad the colour will change rapidly. Make a statement about the freshness of each of the four samples based on your results.

2 Ask your teacher to identify how old each sample of milk was.

3 Why do you think the resazurin test is used regularly by the Milk Marketing Board?

4 What results would you expect if you carried out the two test on
  (a) raw milk staight from the cow
  (b) sterilised milk
  (c) 'live' yoghurt
  (d) evaporated or condensed milk?

5 There has been a lot of discussion recently about the sale of raw milk and the manufacture of unpasteurised cheese. Many small dairy farmers claim that their milk is perfectly safe straight from the cow and that it is quite safe to make cheese from it. The Government is considering making both these practices illegal. What do you think?

Attainment
Target 7
**MAKING NEW
MATERIALS**

Level 7

PRACTICAL 27

Protecting Materials

Metals such as steel, aluminium and copper are easily corroded by water, oxygen, and chemicals in the air. They can be protected by being coated or plated with other metals. Iron is often galvanised by being coated in zinc or plated with chromium. Chromium plating is done by electrolysis.

In this experiment you are going to predict which metals will protect steel against rusting and to test those predictions.

Predictions

You know the reactivity order of the metals to be used in this investigation. Complete the prediction column in the table shown below.

Tube	Metal protecting nail	Prediction rust/ no rust	Appearance of metals	
			End of lesson	Next lesson
1	-			
2	zinc (Zn)			
3	copper (Cu)			
4	tin (Sn)			
5	magnesium (Mg)			
6	lead (Pb)			

Equipment

- □ six boiling tubes
- □ boiling tube rack
- □ five steel nails
- □ salt solution
- □ strips of zinc, copper, tin, magnesium, lead

Procedure

1 Label the test tubes 1 to 6. Clean all the nails and strips of metal using emery paper.
2 Put a nail in tube 1. Pour in salt solution until about half the nail is covered.

3 Wrap the end of the strip of zinc round the middle of a nail. Make sure it is firmly joined. Put this in tube 2.

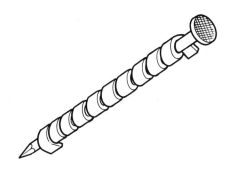

4 Pour in salt solution until it just covers the zinc. The end of the nail should be out of the salt solution.
5 Repeat steps 3 and 4 using the other three metals instead of zinc.
6 Leave the tubes set up at least until the next lesson.

Results

Record the appearance of the nails and the metal wrapped around each of them. Say if a chemical reaction appears to have taken place.

Discussion

1 Compare your predictions with the results and write down where they agreed and where they disagreed.

2 Is there a pattern which links your results and the reactivity order of the metals? Describe it if there is.

3 Find out what is meant by a sacrificial anode and why zinc is one of the most commonly used metals for the prevention of corrosion.

Attainment
Target 8
**EXPLAINING
HOW
MATERIALS
BEHAVE**
Level 9

PRACTICAL 28
Radioactivity and Living Things

Radiation is all around us, but – apart from visible light – we cannot detect it without special apparatus. Some of it is called ionising radiation, and that can affect living matter. In this experiment you will investigate the effect of radiation on living seeds.

You will be provided with some tomato or barley seeds that have been irradiated. Each set of seeds will have been treated by different amounts of radiation, e.g. 0, 5, 10, 25, 50 and 100 units.

Equipment

- yoghurt pot
- compost
- seeds – normal and irradiated

Procedure

1 Your teacher will allocate a seed sample to your group. Make a note of the radiation dose this sample has received. Take 20 seeds.
2 Take a yoghurt pot and make a series of small holes in its base. Half fill the pot with potting compost then scatter the seeds on the surface of the compost.
3 Lightly cover the seeds with more compost and water them.
4 Label the pot with the radiation dose, then leave it in a warm place.
5 Examine your pot, and those of other groups (who will have been given seeds with different radiation doses), every 2 days. Note the number of seeds germinating; how long the shoots are; how many leaves they have and what the seedlings look like. Continue for about 28 days.
6 Do not forget to water the seeds regularly.

Results

Collect a complete set of results from your class and present them in the form of a table.

Presentation

Draw a block graph to show how the germination of the seeds varied according to the radiation dose each batch received.

Discussion

1 Which seeds germinated most rapidly?

2 Does the evidence from your results suggest that the radiation doses the seeds had already received affected their germination?

3 How can you be sure that any differences are not due to other factors?

4 Is it possible to draw any conclusions from your results about the effect of radiation on living organisms? Explain your answer.

5 Can this radiation have other uses? Think about the uses that food manufacturers and surgeons might have for this radiation.

Radon is a natural radioactive gas which, for particular geological reasons, seeps from the ground in certain parts of the country. Radon gas may be responsible for 2500 lung cancer deaths each year. It is estimated that radon and its breakdown products account for half the annual average exposure to ionising radiation in Britain. The average exposure is put at 2.5 millisieverts (mSv) a year. A dose of 20 mSv is considered a cause for action.

6 Scientists talk of 'safe' doses of radiation. What does this phrase mean to you?

7 List all the possible sources of radiation to which you could be exposed. How could you check whether you had received doses in excess of the 'safe' dose?

Attainment
Target 8
**EXPLAINING
HOW
MATERIALS
BEHAVE**
Level 6

PRACTICAL 29

Getting into Hot Water

Problem

It was suggested by a pupil in a science class that if the equipment shown on this page was set up, the water inside the test tube would never boil, no matter how long the water in the beaker was heated. Some pupils agreed and some disagreed.

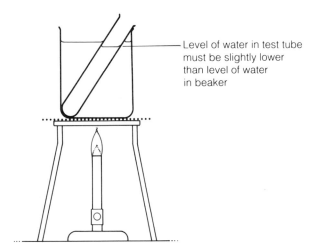

Level of water in test tube must be slightly lower than level of water in beaker

Prediction

1 What do you think? Discuss the problem in your group and write down a prediction. Support your prediction with some reasons.
2 Set up the equipment to test your prediction. How will you know if the water in the tube is boiling? Decide what you will measure or look for.

Equipment

□ 250 cm³ beaker   □ gauze

□ test tube   □ Bunsen burner

□ tripod   □ thermometers

Results

Write a short statement which describes what you found.

Discussion

1 Did you correctly predict what happened?

2 Discuss the problem within your group and try to find an explanation of what happened.

3 Someone suggests that one sure way of getting the water in the test tube to boil is to make the water in the beaker boil at over 100 °C. How might you do this?

4 Test this prediction and write another report.

Attainment
Target 9
**EARTH AND
ATMOSPHERE**

Level 6

PRACTICAL 30

Limestone

Limestone and chalk are both rocks that contain calcium carbonate. They were produced millions of years ago from the shells and skeletons of small marine animals and plants. The amount of calcium carbonate in each type of rock varies.

In this experiment you will investigate the amount of calcium carbonate in samples of these rocks.

Equipment

□ three crucibles

□ hammer

□ piece of cloth

□ piece of wood

□ electric balance

□ kiln (if available)

□ samples of limestone, crushed chalk, calcium carbonate powder

Procedure

1 Take a small quantity of limestone chips. Wrap them in cloth and then, placing them on a piece of scrap wood, use a hammer to crush them into smaller pieces.
2 Take a small amount of natural chalk (not blackboard chalk, which is calcium sulphate). Crush this into smaller pieces.
3 Mark three crucibles L, CH, CC and measure the mass of each precisely.
4 Add about 10 g of crushed limestone (L), crushed chalk (CH) and calcium carbonate powder (CC) to each of the separate crucibles.
5 Measure the new mass of each crucible and its contents.
6 Heat the crucibles to a very high temperature in a kiln (try the art department); a thorough roasting with a Bunsen burner is an alternative.
7 Allow the crucibles to cool. Measure their new masses.
8 Now calculate the loss in mass of the limestone, chalk and calcium carbonate.

Results

Fill in the table.

	Limestone	Chalk	Calcium carbonate
mass of crucible + rock (g)			
mass of crucible + roasted rock (g)			
loss in mass of rock (g)			
mass of crucible alone (g)			
original mass of rock (g)			

Calculate the percentage (%) loss in mass of each of the limestone, chalk and pure calcium carbonate.

$$\% \text{ loss} = \frac{\text{loss in mass (g)}}{\text{original mass (g)}} \times 100\%$$

Discussion

1 List the three materials in order of their percentage content of calcium carbonate.

2 Work out whether limestone or chalk contains the most calcium carbonate ($CaCO_3$).

3 Write a balanced equation to show what happens when calcium carbonate is strongly heated.

4 Why do these materials lose mass when heated?

5 How could you be certain that they have lost their maximum amount of mass?

ESSENTIAL SCIENCE ACTIVITIES   © K. Bishop, W. Scott, D. Maddocks, 1990

Attainment
Target 9
**EARTH AND
ATMOSPHERE**

Level 5

PRACTICAL 31

Hard Rocks

There are three main types of rock:

Igneous. These have been formed from molten material inside the Earth. This material rises through the Earth until it crystallises to form solid rocks. Some molten material can reach the surface and can pour or be blown out of volcanoes. Examples are: granite and gabbro.

Sedimentary. These have been formed from existing rocks on the Earth's surface which have been broken down by the weather and deposited somewhere else. Gradually, over the years the rock particles are cemented or welded together to form a new kind of rock. Examples are: sandstone and limestone.

Metamorphic. These are formed from existing rocks by changes in temperature and pressure. These form new rocks with different appearance and properties. Examples are: slate and marble.

Your tasks are to describe a collection of rocks, and investigate one of their most important properties – density.

Equipment

□ balance
□ hand lens

□ samples of the three types of rocks

Procedure

1 Look at the rocks you have. You might find a hand lens helpful. Try to describe them in as much detail as you can. You might look at whether the rock is coloured; whether it is made of crystals – if so, how big they are; whether each rock contains one substance or more than one – and so on. You decide in your group what to investigate.
2 One of the important properties that a rock has is its density – how much mass it has for a given volume. Your rocks will come in all shapes and sizes and you will not be able to tell with certainty whether one is denser than another – although you might get a 'feel' for it by picking the rocks up. Do this, and see if you can put the rocks in order of increasing density.

To find out the density of anything, you divide its mass by its volume. Finding the mass of each rock is easy – you use a balance. But what about the volume? How will you measure that? Think about this in your group, and make a plan. Then consult your teacher before you begin.

Results

1 Draw up an illustrated report of your investigations of the appearance of the rocks.

2 Look up the densities of the rocks in a data book so that you can identify the samples from their densities.

3 Comment on how accurate your predictions were about the rocks' densities.

Discussion

1 From your investigation of the rocks, what can you say about the properties that each of the rocks might have? Write down as much as you can.

2 The average density of the Earth is 5.5 g cm^{-3}. The actual density of different rocks in the Earth varies greatly. Do you think that rocks found near the surface of the Earth are likely to be more or less dense than those found deep inside the Earth? Give your reasons.

3 The Earth has a radius of 6370 km. Use the information from question 2, and the data you got from your density measurements to estimate what the density of the rocks deep inside the Earth might be.

Attainment
Target 10
FORCES

Level 6

PRACTICAL 32

Bones as Levers

In this practical you will design an experiment to investigate the way that a particular set of bones operate as a lever system in the body.

There are three orders of levers.

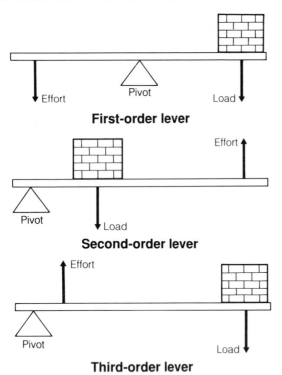

First-order lever

Second-order lever

Third-order lever

In each case the pivot (fulcrum), the load force and the effort force are in different positions. The raising of the forearm is an example of a third-order lever in operation. This is the lever system you will investigate.

The elbow is the pivot, the weight of the forearm and hand is the load force and the pull of the biceps is the effort force.

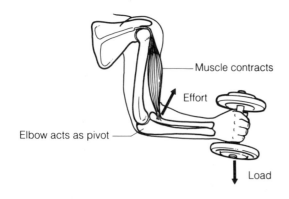

Design

The amount of effort needed to raise a particular load in a lever system depends on how far away the effort force is applied from the pivot point. Work in small groups, using equipment from the list, or any other that is available, and design an experiment to test whether the effort force needed does depend on the distance from the pivot.

If it is true, you will need to say what the relationship is and whether you can express it in a simple way. Work in small groups and discuss your ideas before you begin.

Equipment

☐ stands
☐ clamps
☐ bosses
☐ wood dowelling

☐ Newton meters
☐ masses
☐ metre rule

Discussion

1 Write a report on your experiment outlining your method and results.

2 Plot a graph of effort force against its distance from the pivot.

3 Repeat the experiment using a different load force to see if you get the same relationship as before.

4 Try an experiment which keeps the effort force the same, but varies the distance of the effort force from the pivot; measure the distance moved by the load. Plot a graph of distance moved by load against its distance from the pivot.

5 What connections are there between your results and the arrangement of the pivot, load and effort forces in the arm? For instance, why have the biceps developed in the forearm very close to the elbow, and why is it usually such a strong muscle?

Modelling Paper Bones

The bones of birds are hollow. In fact, no vertebrate animal has solid bones. At first sight this would seem to be a disadvantage as solid bones might appear to be stronger. But is this true?

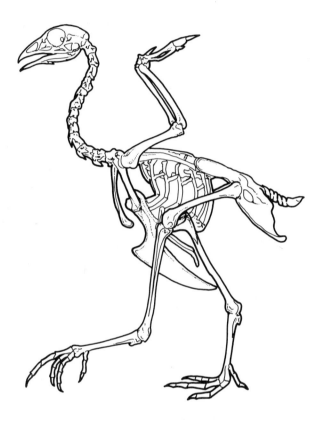

In this experiment you will design and test a variety of paper structures which represent bones. You will compare the relative strengths of hollow and solid tubes with different diameters.

Design

Work in small groups. Choose equipment from the list and any other equipment that is available, and design an experiment that will test the strength of hollow and solid paper tubes. Factors to bear in mind are:

   (a) the thickness of the paper in the tube
   (b) its length
   (c) its diameter.

Discuss your ideas before you start with the rest of the group and agree on a procedure.

Equipment

- ☐ sheets of paper
- ☐ dowelling of various diameters
- ☐ masses and hangers
- ☐ stands, clamps and bosses
- ☐ cotton
- ☐ sticky tape

Discussion

1 Write a report on your experiment. Include the method, use diagrams and record your results in a table.

2 Devise ways in which to represent your results graphically or pictorially.

3 Which type of tube showed greatest strength?

4 What alterations do you need to make to improve your experimental design?

5 Is it reasonable to draw any conclusions about bone strength from your results? Explain your answer.

6 What are the advantages to animals in having hollow bones?

7 Do you think the paper rods can fairly represent the bones of any kind of animal? Explain your answer.

The Efficiency of Pulleys

Pulleys are simple machines used in many places of work. Because they are simple machines they are easy to study.
In this experiment you will investigate the efficiency of these machines.

Equipment

- pulleys
- masses
- Newton meter
- string

Procedure

1 The diagram shows the apparatus needed.

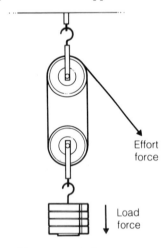

2 Set up the pulley system using two one-track pulleys.
3 Put a known mass on the bottom pulley.
4 Use a Newton meter (spring balance) to measure the effort needed to just lift the load.
5 Repeat the experiment using twice the original load, then three times the load, and so on. Calculate the efficiency each time.
6 Repeat the experiment using a three-track pulley system and then a four-track pulley system.

Results

Record your results in a table such as this:

Load (N)	Effort (N)	Load / Effort x no. of pulleys	Efficiency (%)

Calculate the efficiency of the pulley system using the equation:

$$\text{efficiency} \atop \text{(\%)} = \frac{\text{load}}{\text{effort} \times \text{number of pulleys}} \times 100$$

Presentation

Plot all the results on one graph of efficiency against load.

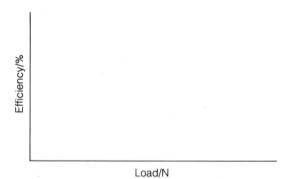

Use the symbols □, × and ○ for the points for the different pulley systems.

Discussion

1 From your graph, how does the efficiency of a pulley system alter as the load gets larger?
2 Think about the mass of the pulley compared to the mass of the load. Why does the efficiency of your pulley systems alter?
3 What is the advantage in using more pulleys in a system?
4 In a single pulley system, the effort force is always greater than the load force. Despite this, single pulley systems are useful. Explain why?

Attainment
Target 11
**ELECTRICITY
AND
MAGNETISM**
Level 5

PRACTICAL 35

Investigating Batteries

Batteries store energy in a chemical form. When the battery is placed in a complete circuit, the chemical energy is changed into electrical energy. There are four main types of battery in common use:
- normal batteries
- high-power batteries
- long-life batteries
- rechargeable alkaline batteries.

It is not necessarily the case that one type of battery is best for all possible uses. But how do you know which one to use?

This experiment begins to investigate the efficiency of these batteries.

Equipment

☐ voltmeter

☐ bulb

☐ 50 cm 26 gauge nichrome resistance wire

☐ connecting leads

☐ 1.5 volt battery

Procedure

1 Work in small groups. Each group will test one of the four kinds of battery.
2 You will be given a fully charged 1.5 volt battery. Note the type you have been given.
3 Make up the circuit as shown in the diagram.

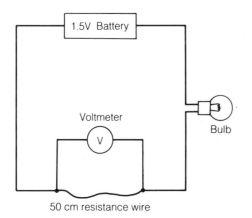

1.5V Battery

Voltmeter

V

Bulb

50 cm resistance wire

4 Take the reading on the voltmeter immediately, and then every 5 minutes until the reading reaches zero.

Results

Collect data from other groups in the class who have used the other kinds of batteries.
Draw a suitable table for the data you have collected.

Presentation

For each battery type, plot the voltage against time on the same piece of graph paper.

Discussion

1 Describe the shape of the curves for the four types of battery. Is there a pattern in the results?

2 What happens to the voltmeter readings in each case? What conclusions can you draw from this?

3 Write a report on the differences between the normal, high-power, and long-life alkaline batteries?

4 Find out the cost of each type of battery. How could you calculate which battery is the best value for money?

5 A rechargeable battery has hidden costs. What must you take into account when you calculate the cost of this type of battery?

6 Which battery would you buy for a torch? Which type of battery would you buy for a cassette tape recorder? Give reasons for your choice.

7 It is claimed that you can 'recharge' a non-rechargeable battery by heating it gently with a fan heater or hair dryer. Design an experiment to investigate this claim. How much extra electrical energy do you get? Is it worth the effort or the cost involved in the 'recharging'?

8 There is no provision for recycling batteries in this country. Why should the disposal of batteries be controlled, as it is in Sweden, and why is it both potentially dangerous and wasteful simply to throw them away? In this country they are either incinerated (burnt at a very high temperature) or dumped in land-fill waste tips along with all other kinds of waste.

9 Batteries are said to be a very wasteful way of storing energy. It takes more energy to make them than they actually provide. Why then do we continue to use them?

Attainment
Target 11
**ELECTRICITY
AND
MAGNETISM**
Level 5

PRACTICAL 36

Fire Alarm Circuit

Fire alarms are designed to detect a large rise in temperature or an increase in smoke levels. They then trigger a warning bell or a sprinkler system.

In this experiment you are going to design a circuit that could be used in a fire alarm.

Equipment

- □ battery or power pack
- □ small candle or wax
- □ laboratory clamp stand
- □ electrical bell
- □ two strips of copper
- □ string or cotton
- □ connecting leads
- □ crocodile clips
- □ paper

Design

1 Work in small groups.
2 Using any equipment from the list, and any other equipment that is available, design a fire alarm. Before you start building the alarm you should discuss your ideas with the other people in the group and agree on a design.
3 Test your design. Is it reliable?
4 Compare your fire alarm with those of other groups.

Discussion

1 Write a report on your fire alarm. Comment on the design in terms of:
(a) sensitivity to heat
(b) reliability
(c) practicality
(d) ingenuity.

2 After seeing other people's alarms, write down how you would change your design in order to improve its sensitivity, practicality and reliability.

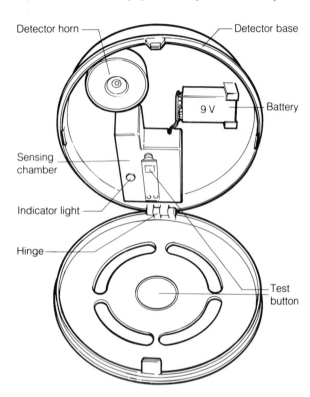

Detector horn — Detector base — Battery (9 V) — Sensing chamber — Indicator light — Hinge — Test button

A modern smoke detector

3 Modern smoke detectors work on a different principle. See if you can find out what this is.

Attainment
Target 11
**ELECTRICITY
AND
MAGNETISM**
Level 7

PRACTICAL 37

Magnetic Effect of an Electric Current

One of the most important discoveries in science was that when an electric current travels along a wire it creates an electromagnetic force around it, just like a bar magnet. The application of this discovery has led to the invention of many useful machines.

The purpose of this practical is to design a simple electromagnet and find out what affects its ability to pick up paper clips.

Equipment

- power pack
- rheostat
- ammeter
- C-bar
- 1 m of insulated wire
- connecting leads
- crocodile clips
- paper clips

Procedure

1 Set up the circuit as shown in the diagram.

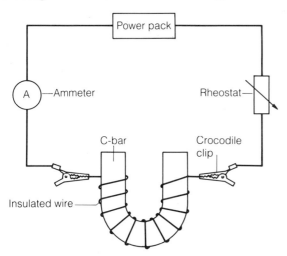

2 Switch the power pack to 2 V.
3 Put ten turns of wire on the C-bar. Switch on the circuit.
4 Adjust the rheostat to give the lowest reading possible on the ammeter. Record that reading.

5 See how many paper clips the C-bar will pick up. Test the electromagnet three times and work out the average number of paper clips it picked up.
6 Repeat the experiment five times, each time increasing the reading on the ammeter by adjusting the rheostat, and counting the number of paper clips picked up by the electromagnet.
7 Repeat the whole experiment using twenty coils of wire.

Results

Use the results table and fill in the average number of paper clips picked up at each current level.

10 turns		1	2	3	4	5
current (amps)						
number of paper clips						

Make a results table for the experiment using twenty coils of wire on the C-bar.

Presentation

Plot a graph of average number of paper clips picked up against the current reading on the ammeter.

Plot the results of the experiment on the same graph for when there were ten turns and when there were twenty turns on the C-bar.

Discussion

1 Describe the shape of the graphs as the current reading was increased. How did the current flowing in the circuit affect the ability of the electromagnet to pick up paper clips?

2 What was the effect of increasing the number of turns on the C-bar?

3 What happens to the paper clips when the circuit is broken? What is the advantage of this over a permanent magnet?

Attainment
Target 11
**ELECTRICITY
AND
MAGNETISM**
Level 7

PRACTICAL 38

Eddy Currents

If a magnet is rotated near a piece of metal it will cause currents to be produced in the metal. These are called eddy currents and they create a weak magnetic field. If the metal is free to move the interaction of the fields will cause it to rotate.

Equipment

- horseshoe magnet
- cork
- small foil dish
- large pin
- cotton

If a horseshoe magnet is not available use two bar magnets separated by a piece of wood, as shown.

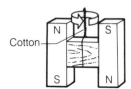

Procedure

1 Put a small dent in the centre of the foil dish. Make a mark somewhere on the edge. Now set up the equipment as shown in the diagram.

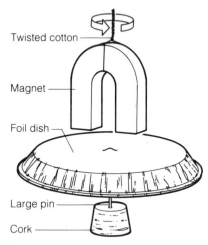

2 Twist the magnet at least twenty times, then release it.
3 Watch what happens.
4 Repeat the procedure with the magnet at different heights above the foil dish. Record what you see.
5 Cut a small piece of plasticine into four equal parts. Space them evenly at the edges underneath the dish. Repeat the procedure and record your observations.

6 Cut the dish in half and tape it together again making sure the metal edges do not come into contact. Repeat the procedure once more.

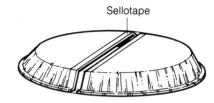

Discussion

1 Write a report about the experiment which includes answers to the following questions.
(a) Did changing the height of the magnet have an effect on the foil dish?
(b) What was the effect of increasing the mass of the dish by adding the pieces of plasticine?
(c) What was the effect when the dish was cut in half and taped back together?
(d) Why was it important for the edges of the two halves not to come into contact?

2 The drawing below is a cut-away diagram of a car speedometer. The faster the car is going the faster the flexible cable rotates.

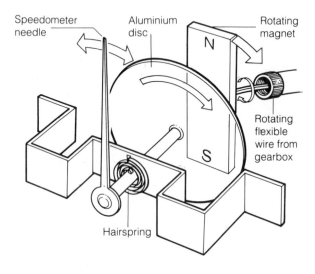

(a) Thinking about your experiment, explain how the speedometer works.
(b) You would expect the speedometer needle to go round and round as well. What prevents this from happening?

3 Look at your electricity meter at home. The same idea is being used – but in reverse. Write a report to explain how the meter disc rotates.

Storing Heat

It is known that different materials do not have the same ability to absorb, and to lose, heat. Night storage heaters are a good example of this. They can store lots of heat overnight taking advantage of cheap electricity. It takes a long time for them to heat up, but by the same token, it takes them a long time to give out their heat – a great advantage.

In this experiment you are going to compare the heat capacities of water, alcohol and paraffin.

Prediction

Would you expect all three liquids to have the same capacity to absorb heat?

Try to predict an order and attempt to come up with a plausible scientific explanation for it.

Equipment

- power pack
- rheostat
- ammeter
- 250 cm³ beaker
- connecting leads
- two crocodile clips
- measuring cylinder
- 30 cm resistance wire
- thermometer
- alcohol, water and paraffin

Procedure

1 For a fair test you must make sure that all the following variables are kept the same:
  (a) volume of the liquid under test
  (b) heating coil
  (c) ammeter reading
  (d) length of time the current is passed.

The only variable that should change in the investigation is the liquid. You then need to measure the temperature reached by each of the three liquids once the above conditions have been set.

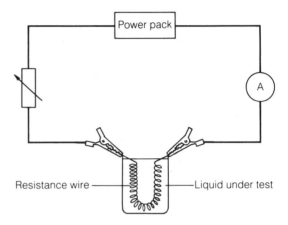

2 Carry out a test run with water to find out which combination of current setting and length of time will give you a reasonable rise in temperature in a fairly short time. Try about 1 amp for between five and ten minutes.
3 Carry out the investigation with each of three liquids. Repeat the experiments to check for consistency.

Results

Draw a bar graph to represent your results.

Discussion

1 Is there a significant difference between the results for the three liquids?

2 Compare the results with your predictions. What similarities or differences are there?

3 If they are different can you suggest any reasons for the results you obtained?

4 Suggest possible practical implications of your findings.

5 Make suggestions as to how the experiment might be improved.

Attainment
Target 13
ENERGY

Level 4

PRACTICAL 40

Energy From Chemicals

Batteries are an extremely useful mobile source of energy. Sadly it takes more energy to make them than you can ever get out of them. Many contain mercury and cadmium, heavy metals which are notoriously toxic when released into the environment. At the moment we do not have any special means of disposing of them or recycling them.

In this experiment you are going to investigate the way batteries work.

Equipment

- two 100 cm³ beakers
- voltmeter
- connecting leads
- two crocodile clips
- filter paper soaked in potassium nitrate solution
- 100 cm³ measuring cylinder

- strips of metal: zinc, magnesium, iron, lead, tin, copper
- solutions of metal salts: zinc sulphate, magnesium sulphate, iron(II) sulphate, lead sulphate, tin(II) chloride, copper(II) sulphate

Procedure

1 Label the beakers A and B.
2 Put a strip of metal and 25 cm³ of the corresponding metal salt solution into beaker A.
3 Put a different metal strip and its corresponding salt solution into beaker B.
4 Connect the two beakers with a strip of filter paper soaked in saturated potassium nitrate.
5 Connect the two strips of metal to the voltmeter and record the voltage.

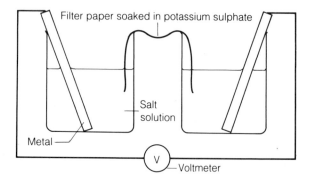

6 Test all possible combinations. Work out the best sequences so that you do not have to change the solutions in both beakers every time. Do not throw the solutions away as they must be reused.

Results

Copy out the headings shown in the table below. Draw a grid which allows each metal and its solution to be connected and tested with each of the other metals and their solutions.

Metal and solution in beaker A	Metal and solution in beaker B	Reading on voltmeter (volts)

Presentation

List the results so that the voltages obtained are in rank order, i.e. highest at the top.

Discussion

1 Look for any obvious patterns in the results and write down what you see.

2 It is known that there is a link between the reactivity of the metals and the voltages obtained from the different combinations. With this in mind and knowing something of the properties of the metals from previous experience, try to use the results to put the metals into an order of reactivity. Put the most reactive metal first.

3 Write out a pattern which describes which combination gives the highest voltages, and which gives the lowest.

4 Carry out research into batteries and write about the following points:
   (a) the difference between wet and dry batteries
   (b) the disadvantages of batteries for storing large amounts of energy, e.g. why electric cars (such as the C5) have not yet been successful
   (c) whether rechargeable batteries are worth the extra money
   (d) why long-life batteries are cost-effective in some uses, but not necessarily in all
   (e) how environment friendly 'green' batteries are.

Releasing Heat Energy

In the last investigation, you looked at ways of obtaining energy from chemicals. The reactants were joined by filter paper and wires, and the energy was released in the form of electricity. This is because the chemicals were reacting 'at a distance'.

It is also possible to obtain energy from these chemicals – but this time in the form of heat. To do this, you have to mix the chemicals together.

Equipment

□ boiling tubes

□ racks for the tubes

□ metals and solutions of metal salts

□ thermometer

□ insulating material such as cotton wool

Procedure

1 Look at your results from *Practical 40 – Energy from Chemicals* and pick the pairs of chemicals which gave you the largest voltages.
2 Using the equipment listed above – and using any other you feel is needed – plan an investigation to see how much heat energy can be obtained from the chemicals.
   You will need to make sure that you use the same amount and concentration of solution each time, and that you use enough metal to react completely with the solution.
   Think about the way chemical reactions occur, and what you can do to make them take place quickly. You want to make sure that these reactions take place as rapidly as possible. What can you do?
3 When you have a plan, consult your teacher about it before you begin.

Results

Present your results in a suitable table.

Discussion

1 What conclusions did you come to about the best way to carry out these reactions?

2 Compare your results with those in the other experiment where you produced electricity. What similarities and differences did you find?

3 What was being produced in your reactions? Write word equations for the reactions which were taking place.

4 Name as many chemical reactions as you can where large amounts of energy can be obtained. How do we use these reactions?

Measuring Energy in Food

Anyone on a diet knows that it is essential to study tables of food energy values – a calorie controlled diet is the phrase you often hear, but how are these energy values calculated?

In this experiment you are going to measure the energy in nuts. Nuts are seeds which are compact little packets of energy from which new plants can grow. You are going to compare the energy values of peanuts with hazelnuts and brazil nuts. By burning them in air and measuring the rise in temperature they cause in a known volume of water, you can calculate their relative energy values.

Equipment

- □ three boiling tubes
- □ mounted needle
- □ 100 cm^3 measuring cylinder
- □ thermometer
- □ electric balance
- □ nuts
- □ clamp stand

Procedure

Before you start you must design the way you are going to carry out the experiment. Each nut must be ignited and burnt in exactly the same way otherwise you will not have data which can be used to compare the energy values of the nut. It is worth doing a trial run first to see what the difficulties are before collecting the data.

1 Measure the mass of one of the nuts to one decimal place.
2 Measure 40 cm^3 (40 g) of cold tap water into a boiling tube.
3 Record the temperature of the tap water.
4 Fix the boiling tube in clamp, boss and stand.
5 Stick a mounted needle into the nut, and hold the nut in a Bunsen flame.
6 As soon as it lights, hold it steadily just below the boiling tube and keep it there until it burns out.
7 Measure the new temperature of the water.
8 Repeat the whole experiment using fresh tap water and another type of nut.

Results

Copy out and complete the table below.

Type of nut	Mass of nut (g)	Temp. before (°C)	Temp. after (°C)	Temp. rise (°C)

To compare the energy value of the nuts you need to calculate their energy values per gram.

$$\text{Energy value of each nut (J)} = \text{mass of water (g)} \times 4.2 \times \text{rise in temperature (°C)}$$

$$\text{Energy value per gram (J/g)} = \frac{\text{energy value (J)}}{\text{mass of nut (g)}}$$

Discussion

1 Set out your calculations clearly and list the nuts in rank order according to their energy values per gram (J/g).

2 Suggest possible reasons why they are not all the same. (Hint: the energy value of fat is twice that of the same mass of protein or carbohydrate.)

3 The figure of 4.2 represents the heat capacity of the water. What is this and what are its units?

4 Describe the problems you found when trying to keep the experiments fair. List the variables and the way you controlled them.

5 Bearing in mind the limitations of laboratory equipment, suggest improvements that could be made if you were to do the experiment again.

6 This experiment is basically the same as that used to work out the sorts of energy value tables you see in magazines, but they give energy values in calories. Explain the link between calories and joules.

Investigating Stereo

Stereo records and tapes aim to produce music that sounds as natural as possible. Each of our ears receives a slightly different sound and our brain is fooled into thinking each different sound comes from a slightly different position. This experiment investigates how our brain locates the direction of sounds using information from our ears.

Procedure

1 You should work in small groups – four is an ideal number. One person should be the subject of the experiment. The subject should be blindfolded or keep their eyes tightly shut. One person should record the results.

2 The rest of the group must work in silence. At intervals of five seconds someone in the group should make a short sharp sound from one of the positions shown.

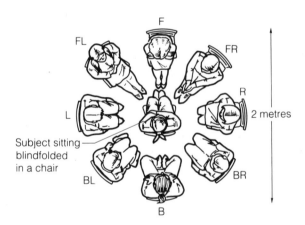

Subject sitting blindfolded in a chair

2 metres

The subject should point to where they thought the sound came from. Note this in the table. Repeat, using different positions.

3 Repeat the experiment, but this time with one ear sealed. Next repeat with the other ear sealed.

4 Repeat the experiment, but with sounds coming from two different directions, at the same time. Record the results in suitable tables such as the one shown here:

	Sound came from							
	L	FL	F	FR	R	BR	B	BL
Subject pointed to								
Number correct								

Discussion:

1 Which positions could the subject pinpoint most accurately?

2 Which positions were hardest to pinpoint?

3 Can you give a reasonable explanation for these results?

4 How did the results alter when only one ear was being used? Was there a difference between the right and left ear?

5 How do you think the brain works out where sounds come from, just by information from the ears?

6 Design an experiment that investigates whether the distance of a sound from the ear affects a person's ability to identify the direction.

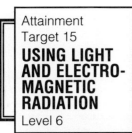

Attainment
Target 15
**USING LIGHT
AND ELECTRO-
MAGNETIC
RADIATION**
Level 6

PRACTICAL 44

The Rainbow Effect

A rainbow is quite a common event, but what causes it? White light is a mixture of electromagnetic waves that the human eye can detect. This mixture can be separated by passing the light through a prism or a spectroscope. The light is then separated into a band of colours that range from red to violet. In this experiment you will investigate the range of colours which we call the visible spectrum.

Equipment

☐ light source
☐ various coloured filters
☐ prism
☐ spectroscope
☐ white and red card

Procedure

1 Arrange a light source and a prism, so that the beam from the source passes through a prism and splits to form a spectrum which then shines onto a white card. Record the array of colours on the card.
2 Arrange a filter in front of the prism, as shown in the diagram.

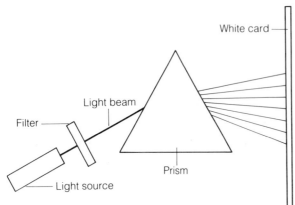

White card
Light beam
Filter
Light source
Prism

Record its effect on the spectrum shining on the card. Repeat using different filters, or combinations of filters. Put your results in a suitable table.

Colour of filter	Effect on spectrum

3 Repeat the experiment, using a spectroscope instead of the prism. Note the effect of using different coloured filters, and combinations of filters, on the spectrum.

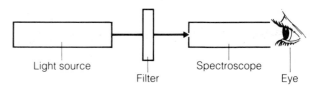

Light source
Filter
Spectroscope
Eye

4 Take a red card. Shine light of different colours onto the card, and note what happens to the apparent colour of the card. Repeat with a blue card and a green card. Record your results in a suitable table.

Actual colour of card	Colour of light	Apparent colour of card

Discussion

1 Why does light passing through a prism split into different bands of colour?

2 How does the action of a spectroscope differ from the action of a prism?

3 What is the effect of a coloured filter on white light? Does the filter remove all the colour?

4 What is the effect of coloured light on coloured card? Does the card's colour seem to change?

5 Many street lights are orange in colour? How will this affect the apparent colour of cars parked near them?

6 Colour films are made for natural sunlight or for artificial floodlights. Light from the Sun is made up of a mixture of colours. What is the difference between sunlight and the light from electric bulbs? Should you use natural light film or artificial light film with a flashgun? What does this tell you about the colour of the flash light?

7 Based on the knowledge you have gained from this experiment, explain what causes sunlight to be split up to form a rainbow.

ESSENTIAL SCIENCE ACTIVITIES © K. Bishop, W. Scott, D. Maddocks, 1990

Attainment
Target 15
**USING LIGHT
AND ELECTRO-
MAGNETIC
RADIATION**
Level 7

PRACTICAL 45

Colour TV

A television has an electron gun which fires a stream of electrons at the screen which is coated with thousands of phosphor dots. These dots glow as the electrons hit them. A colour television has three different electron guns and three different types of phosphor dots, one for each of the colours red, green and blue. These are the only three colours that are actually produced on the screen – our brain is fooled into seeing the complete range of colours because of an optical illusion. In this experiment you will investigate the production of colours on a television screen.

Equipment

- □ colour television
- □ magnifying glass
- □ 3 ray boxes or light sources
- □ red, green and blue filters

Procedure

1 Turn on a colour television set. Use a magnifying glass to study a small area of the screen. Draw a simple diagram to show the dots or stripes that you can see. Do not look at the screen for more than a few minutes!

2 Set up three ray boxes or light sources as shown in the diagram.

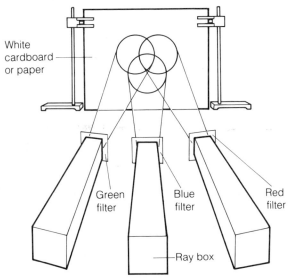

White cardboard or paper

Green filter

Blue filter

Red filter

Ray box

Put a different coloured filter in front of each of them. Shine the light from the light sources so that the light beams overlap as shown.

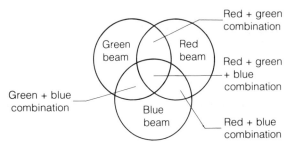

Green beam

Red beam

Red + green combination

Red + green + blue combination

Green + blue combination

Blue beam

Red + blue combination

3 Complete the table showing the colours produced when the red, green and blue light beams mix.

Filter combination	Colour seen on paper
red + blue	
red + green	
green + blue	
red + green + blue	

4 Alter the brightness of one of the images by moving one of the lamps further away (or by reducing its electrical current if you can). Describe what happens to the colours on the screen.

Discussion

1 If all the beams are of the same intensity, how many colours can be produced by the red, green and blue lamps?

2 If the intensity of the beams can be altered, how many colours can be produced by the red, green and blue lamps?

3 The intensity of the electron beams from each of the three electron guns in a colour television can be altered independently of each other. How many colours can be produced by these three electron guns?

4 How is the colour black produced on a colour TV screen?

5 What are the major differences between a normal colour TV and a Sony Trinitron screen? Explain the reason for these differences?

6 If coloured paints are mixed, different colours are produced. Try mixing the following paints to see what colours are produced:

red + green =
green + blue =
blue + red =
red + green + blue =

Compare the colours you get with the ones produced by mixing coloured light. Explain the differences.

Attainment
Target 15
**USING LIGHT
AND ELECTRO-
MAGNETIC
RADIATION**
Level 6

PRACTICAL 46

Sight Defects

People who cannot focus clearly on distant objects are said to be short-sighted. Short-sighted people hold books very close to their face in order to focus on the print. Long-sight causes difficulty focusing on near objects. People with this defect will tend to hold things away from themselves in order to see clearly. In this experiment you will investigate the type of lenses that can be used to correct these two conditions.

Equipment

□ light source   □ white card (screen)

□ wire grid as object

□ convex and concave
  lenses of various focal
  length

Procedure

1 Set up the equipment as shown in the diagram.

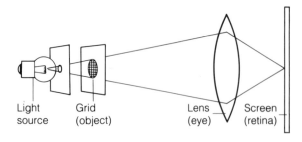

Light   Grid   Lens   Screen
source   (object)   (eye)   (retina)

2 Adjust the position of the lens and screen until the object is clearly focussed on the screen by the lens. This represents normal sight.
3 Move the screen further away from the lens so that the object is out of focus. This represents short-sightedness.

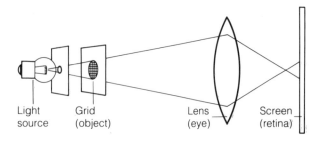

Light   Grid   Lens   Screen
source   (object)   (eye)   (retina)

4 Keeping the screen in this position take a lens and put it between the object and the eye lens.
  Move this lens back and forth and try to bring the object back into focus. Repeat the process until you find a lens that works. Make a note of the type of lens it is.
5 Set up the normal position again. Then bring the screen towards the lens so that the object again is just out of focus. This represents long-sightedness.

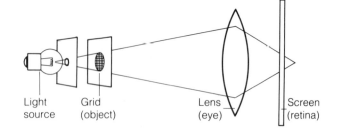

Light   Grid   Lens   Screen
source   (object)   (eye)   (retina)

6 Again sort through a variety of lenses and try them in various positions between the object and lens until the object is brought back into focus. Describe the type of lens that you found successful.

Discussion

1 The lenses you were using represent spectacles or contact lenses. What sort of lens corrected
(a) short-sight?
(b) long-sight?

2 As a model of the human eye the apparatus has serious drawbacks. What do you think they are?

3 As people get older the lens in the eye often becomes inflexible. Such people need spectacles particularly for reading and looking at near objects. What sort of lens would be best suited for them?

4 Many people decide to change from wearing spectacles to contact lenses. What reasons can you think of for making this change?

Attainment
Target 15
**USING LIGHT
AND ELECTRO-
MAGNETIC
RADIATION**
Level 6

PRACTICAL 47

Investigating Sunglasses

There are four common types of sunglasses. These have lenses which are:
- tinted
- reflective (mirrored glasses)
- polaroid
- photoreactive.

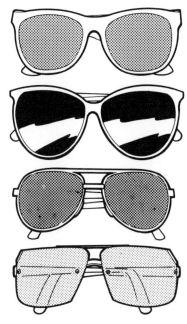

All these glasses work in different ways, but they all have the same aim – to reduce the amount of light reaching the eye. In this experiment you will design a method of investigating the efficiency of each type of sunglasses.

Equipment

- ☐ torch or projector (or light source, e.g window on a sunny day)
- ☐ polaroid sunglasses
- ☐ tinted sunglasses
- ☐ photoreactive sunglasses
- ☐ reflective sunglasses

Design

1 Work in small groups. Choose the equipment from the list, and any other that is available, and design a method of testing the efficiency of each type of sunglasses.
2 Discuss your ideas with the others in your group and agree on an experimental design before you start.

Discussion

1 Write a report on your experiment. In your report you should outline your method and your results.
Discuss how you would modify the experimental design if you were to repeat your investigation.

2 Which pair of sunglasses was most efficient? Explain what you understood by the meaning of efficiency, as far as sunglasses are concerned.

3 Which type of sunglasses would you buy? Explain the reasons for your choice.

4 Discuss the advantages and disadvantages of each type of sunglasses by considering the following points:
    (a) look at the way each type is advertised.
    (b) how is each type described?
    (c) what are the major points made in these adverts?
    (d) are the claims justified?

Attainment
Target 15
**USING LIGHT
AND ELECTRO-
MAGNETIC
RADIATION**
Level 10

PRACTICAL 48
Investigating Polarised Light

Light is a form of electromagnetic energy that is produced when electrons vibrate. These vibrations produce waves which move in all directions. They are called transverse waves. In a beam of normal light the transverse waves can be moving in all directions. Some materials will cut out all of these transverse wave directions except one. Materials, such as polaroid filters, produce a type of light that is called polarised light. In this experiment you will investigate this light.

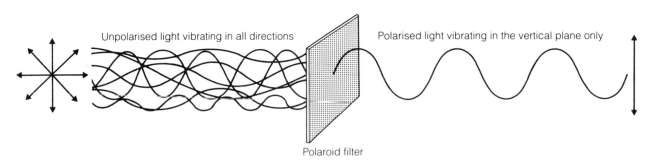

Unpolarised light vibrating in all directions

Polarised light vibrating in the vertical plane only

Polaroid filter

Equipment

- □ sticky tape
- □ thin transparent plastic (e.g. OHP film) or glass
- □ two polaroid filters or two pairs of polaroid sunglasses

Procedure

1 Hold one of the polaroid filters in front of a light source such as a window. Look through the filter and record its effect on light intensity.
2 Take the second filter and place it in front of the first. Hold both the filters up to the light, then slowly rotate one of the filters. Record its effect on the light.
3 Take the piece of plastic and add a series of layers of sticky tape, as shown in the diagram.
4 Put one of the polaroid filters in front of this plastic film, and the other behind the plastic. Hold this plastic 'sandwich' up to the light. Record the effect on the light.
5 Rotate one of the pieces of polaroid through 90 degrees. As this is being done look at the light coming through the 'sandwich'.

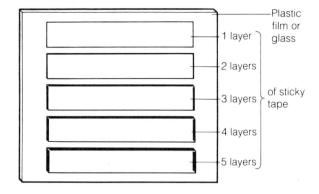

Plastic film or glass

1 layer
2 layers
3 layers } of sticky tape
4 layers
5 layers

Discussion

1 Explain what happens when two polaroid filters are rotated in front of a light source.

2 Sticky tape has the property of slightly twisting the polarised light beam. Try to explain the effects of the different layers of sticky tape on polarised light. Do you think that this property has any use?

3 Some anglers use polaroid sunglasses when fishing. Photographers often use a polaroid filter when taking photographs of the sky. Try to explain how these filters are useful in these circumstances.

Measuring the Moon

The Moon is the largest object in the night sky. People have always been fascinated by it, and some scientists think that Stonehenge was used as a lunar observatory. There have been many attempts to measure its size and its distance from the Earth. The most recent attempts used laser beams which were reflected off a special dish left on the Moon by American astronauts. The lasers measured the distance from the Earth to the Moon with an accuracy of a few centimetres. But how big is the Moon? This experiment shows you one way that you can estimate its diameter.

Equipment

□ metre rule or rod □ Plasticine/Blu-tac

□ 1p coin

Procedure

1 Wait for a clear night with a full, or almost full, Moon.
2 Take a long straight rod, a 1p coin and a small amount of Plasticine or Blu-tac.
3 Support the rod and look along it towards the Moon. Slide the coin backwards and forwards until it just hides the Moon.

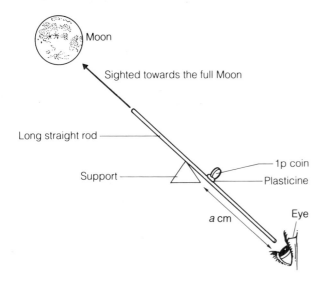

4 Note the distance in cm (a) of the coin from your eye and record it in the table.
5 Repeat this five times and take the average value of (a).

Trial number	a (cm)
1	
2	
3	
4	
5	
Average value	

Results

Calculate the diameter of the Moon using the following information:
  (a) The diameter of a 1p coin is 2 cm.
  (b) The average distance of the Moon from the Earth is 380 000 km.

Watch the units in the calculation!

$$\text{Hint:} \quad \frac{2}{a} = \frac{\text{Moon diameter}}{\text{distance from the Moon}}$$

$$\text{Moon diameter} = \frac{2 \times 380\,000}{a} \text{ km}$$

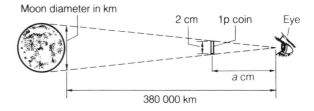

Discussion

1 What difficulties did you face in this experiment? What did you do to overcome them? What were the major sources of error? Try to express them as percentages.

2 Look at the size of the Moon's diameter in a reference book. Now work out how accurate your answer was.

3 The distance of the Earth from the Moon is not constant because of the effect of the other planets in the Solar System, particularly Jupiter. Can you explain why Jupiter should have such an effect? Use sketches to illustrate your answer.

4 When the Moon eclipses the Sun it usually just covers the face of the Sun. This means that the angle the Sun makes to the eye is the same as that of the Moon. If the Sun is about 150 million km away from us, work out its diameter.

Attainment
Target 17
**THE NATURE
OF SCIENCE**

Level 5

PRACTICAL 50

Making Observations

Chemists are often asked to identify substances. To do this they need to know something about the chemical reactions of substances similar to the ones they are investigating. Compounds which have metals in them often react in similar ways. So sometimes you can guess what is in a compound from the way it reacts with other compounds.

The purpose of this experiment is to test your ability to make careful and accurate observations and then to use those observations to make decisions.

You will be given a number of labelled chemicals and several unknown ones. The aim is to compare the reactions of the unknown chemicals with the reactions of the known ones.

You have to judge which metal you think is contained in each unknown.

Equipment

- □ two racks and six boiling tubes
- □ six known solutions
  Cobalt(II) chloride
  Iron(II) sulphate
  Copper(II) sulphate
  Zinc sulphate
  Iron(II) chloride
- □ several unknown solutions marked A,B, C, etc.
- □ test reagent sodium hydroxide – handle with care.

Procedure

1 Set up six boiling tubes in racks. Label each one with the name of one of the six known chemical solutions.

2 Carefully pour exactly 3 cm depth of each of the six liquids into the correspondingly labelled boiling tubes.
3 Add five drops (no more) of test reagent sodium hydroxide into each boiling tube and make accurate notes of everything you see.
4 Now top up each tube to 5 cm with more sodium hydroxide and again record exactly what happens.
5 Thoroughly rinse out all the boiling tubes.
6 Now you must test the unknowns (3 cm depth as before) with, firstly, five drops of sodium hydroxide and secondly, topped up to 5 cm depth with sodium hydroxide.

Results

Design a table which will be large enough to hold all the information you obtained from the reactions just carried out.

Discussion

1 For each of the unknown chemicals try to find one of the standards which appears to give similar results. If there is doubt go for the one that seems to be the closest. If there is no similarity whatsoever – then record that.

2 For each unknown, say which metal you think it contains based on the evidence of your results.

PRACTICAL 51
Gathering Evidence and Drawing Conclusions

Every scientist has to make judgements based on the evidence obtained from experiments. Often evidence is not one hundred per cent conclusive and decisions have to be made on the balance of the evidence, that is, on what seems to be reasonable.

The purpose of this experiment is to carry out a series of tests to find out which of the liquids A, B, C, D or E is most likely to be pure water.

Information

1 Pure water should have a pH of 7 (neutral).
2 Pure water sometimes contains a little dissolved CO_2 which makes it acidic.
3 Water will turn blue cobalt chloride from blue to pink or white.
4 When heated, pure water will leave no residue.
  Beware – some liquids look like water but when heated are dangerous – inflammable.
5 White copper sulphate turns blue when water is added to it.
  Note – you will have to make white $CuSO_4$ by heating a small amount of the blue crystals in a test tube.
  Beware – let it cool before adding any test liquids.
6 Pure water has a boiling point of exactly 100 °C.
7 Inflammable liquids often have a strong smell.
  Beware – do not stick a tube directly under your nose. Use the proper technique if you wish to smell a liquid.

Procedure

Carry out as many tests as possible based on these facts, to build up a body of evidence. Do not jump to conclusions. Do not carry out dangerous tests.

The skills being looked for in the procedure are:
1 Safety – use of apparatus and handling of chemicals must be carried out with safety uppermost in mind. (Only carry out test based on fact 6 if you are sure it's safe.)
2 Good organisation – ensure that you work efficiently and do not do unnecessary tests. Plan the order of your tests before you start.

Results

Design a table which will be large enough for the observations you have collected.

Discussion

1 Study your results carefully and decide which of the liquids could be pure water. Explain your reasons.

2 For the other liquids write down one piece of evidence which made you decide that the liquid could not possibly be water.

3 Which of the liquids are you not sure about? Say why there is some doubt in your mind.

4 Write a paragraph which describes the characteristics of pure water.